MAKE WORK
WORK FOR YOU

ISBN: 978-1-77995-014-7
e-ISBN: 978-1-77995-015-4

First edition, first impression 2024

Published by Bookstorm (Pty) Ltd
PO Box 296
Riebeek Kasteel
Western Cape
7307
South Africa
www.bookstorm.co.za

Edited by Tracey Hawthorne
Proofread by Janet Bartlet
Cover and book design by Dogstar Design

MAKE WORK WORK FOR YOU

Judy Klipin

BOOK**STORM**

Judy Klipin was born in Johannesburg, South Africa, where she continues to live with her family. Judy specialises in working with people who are experiencing burnout and people who had challenging childhoods (adult children); more often than not these are the same people.

Judy combines her knowledge and skills as a Martha Beck Certified Master Life Coach and a Transactional Analysis practitioner to teach her clients simple, practical and powerful tools that help them to change – not who they are, but how they are – so that they can make their work and their lives work better for them. She coaches, mentors and trains individuals and groups, both in person and online.

Judy has a BA and HDipED from the University of the Witwatersrand and a Masters in Social Sciences from Leicester University.

Other books by Judy Klipin:
Recover from Your Childhood: Life Lessons for the Adult Child (Bookstorm 2019)
Recover from Burnout: Life Lessons to Regain Your Passion and Purpose (Bookstorm 2019)
Life Lessons for the Adult Child (Penguin Books 2011)

Find out more at www.judyklipin.com.

Contents

Introduction: Work should work for us

Once upon a time I worked for six very long and very unhappy months in an office that had no natural light or air. There was one window in the entire place – and that window had been painted over and sealed shut.

I am a person who needs to see the sun and the sky and the trees. I need to hear the birds and smell the grass. It was very depressing for me to be in an air-conditioned, artificially lit environment.

Also, my boss – who was not someone I had anything in common with – would keep the air-conditioning set at arctic temperatures because she found the cold air 'invigorating'. I used to have to wear winter clothes in the heat of summer.

I liked the other two staff members, but the boss-lady liked to keep us apart from each other so there was very little opportunity for conversation or connection.

All of this would have been more bearable if the work I was doing had been in any way interesting, rewarding or meaningful. But it wasn't any of these things. It was boring and mostly menial, and there wasn't enough of it to keep me occupied for more than a couple of hours every long day.

The environment made me unhappy. So did the work (or lack thereof) itself. And the person I worked for. And the loneliness. And the feeling of spending my precious time doing nothing worthwhile.

I got sick. A lot. And the longer I stayed there, the more miserable I became, and the more my migraines and stomach issues evolved. And the sicker and more miserable I became, the less able I was to imagine a better working future, and the more stuck I felt.

In retrospect, it is pretty clear that one of the major reasons I stayed was because I needed to earn money to pay for my therapy. I was in therapy because I was depressed, and I was depressed because of where I was working…

Every day I thought about quitting (not quietly – my fantasies involved a very public, very dramatic departure that would leave no observer in any doubt as to how awful I found the whole experience), but as soon as I had decided to hand in my resignation, I would remember how long it had taken me to find the job, and how soul-destroying the search had been.

I was caught in the nowhere-land of hating where I was, and being overwhelmingly anxious about not being able to find anywhere else to be.

Had I had been less worn down and dejected by the place, and had I been able to afford a coach – not that non-sport coaching was even a thing back then – I would have managed to do exactly what I hope this book will help you to do: identify and describe all the elements of my work that weren't working for me, and make a plan to improve them.

In an ideal world, we would all be doing work we love, with people we get along with and in places that spark only joy. However, we are very far away from that ideal and not likely to reach it any time soon. Many people do not have the luxury of finding jobs that make them jump with jubilation.

The most distressing reason for someone coming to me for coaching is when they feel so defeated by their situation and so unable to change or improve it that they resign themselves to it – they accept a bad situation that cannot be changed. They drag themselves to work, through work and back home again every day. It is a different kind of Great Resignation, and is a major contributor to the burnout epidemic we are currently experiencing.

The Great Resignation is an economic trend that began in early 2021 in the wake of the Covid-19 pandemic, in which a huge wave of employees voluntarily resigned from their jobs. The reasons for resigning included wage stagnation, hostile work environments, inflexible remote-work policies and job dissatisfaction. Literally millions of people who had the opportunity to do so handed in their notice and left their jobs for greener, or certainly different, pastures.

And the Great Return, when companies brought their employees back to the office after months and sometimes years of remote work, took many people back to environments which, challenging as they were before the pandemic, had become almost intolerable after the respite of the distance afforded by the lockdowns.

Unfortunately, with the economy being what it is, more and more people are having to stay in situations that are not optimal for them. They are relieved to have a job at all, even if it is far removed from what they dreamed about when preparing for employment – even if they have to work for a horrible boss, or with toxic people, or in a place that generates the opposite of joy. The challenges of unfulfilling work are often outweighed by the benefits of being gainfully employed.

In these circumstances, it is important that we are able to make the changes we can in order to make the work we have work for us, so that we can keep paying our bills and meeting our financial and social commitments.

So, what do we do when we hate our work but have to stay with and in it to survive? We may not be able to love everything about our work, but with some effort and attention, we can find some aspects of it to love – or at least to feel warmly towards. This book aims to help you to do that, while also helping you to change what you can so that you loathe the rest of it less.

Coaching is all about helping clients to understand that they have choices.

Even if it doesn't always feel like it, almost every adult has a choice about how they respond to the situations in which they find themselves. One of the most pleasing parts of my work is helping people to find a sense of hope for change and a realisation that despite possibly not being able to change *if* they stay in a situation, they can change *how* they are while they stay there.

My hope is that this book will help you to identify what you'd like to change, and provide some practical tools and guidance that will help you to make those changes to make work work better for you – whatever and wherever your work may be.

Over the chapters that follow, we will build up your toolbox so that you are not only able to identify what is broken but will also have the means to make the necessary repairs. You will become aware and prepared to improve what isn't working well for you, and to make what is already good even better. I will be sharing many case studies* and tools so that you will finish this book fully equipped to solve almost any problem you encounter.

* All the subjects of the case studies have given permission for their stories to be told. Even so, I have taken great care to change all identifying information. If you feel you recognise yourself or someone else in the stories, it is because they have been chosen for the universal truths and experiences they offer.

Where are you now?

Before you can make work work better for you, you need to establish what about it isn't working so well.

Many of my clients know that they are unhappy at work but they aren't entirely sure why. This makes them feel that *all* of work is the problem, rather than seeing that it is in all likelihood only *some aspects* of work that are creating the unhappiness.

Once we know what isn't working, it is much easier to come up with a solution. But, often, the hardest part is identifying the problem. By breaking the whole of work down into some of its smaller parts, it is relatively easy to see where the problems and discomforts are, and to decide how to address them.

The Wheel of Work

The Wheel of Work is a useful model to measure where you are needing to pay attention by helping you to create a visual map of how satisfied you are in each area of your work life. This exercise will probably serve to confirm what you already know (where you feel that work is working for you and where it isn't), and it will also, in combination with the chapters that follow, give some insight into why some areas of your work are feeling more or less satisfying.

The Wheel of Work presents eight key areas of work. All are interrelated and influence each other. Although it is an artificial separation to create eight silos – work, like life, is systemic in nature, with all elements affecting and being affected by each other – creating main themes and areas is the most effective way of identifying, thinking about and addressing the myriad possible problems and issues that arise at work.

The Wheel of Work will help you to assess how satisfied you currently feel in each of these areas of work. It will provide you with a helicopter view of your personal work system, and where and how you may be out of balance. Each area is explored and unpacked in the eight chapters that follow; various elements of the area are discussed, and case studies and activities are presented to enhance your understanding of your work experience, while giving you skills to make it work better for you.

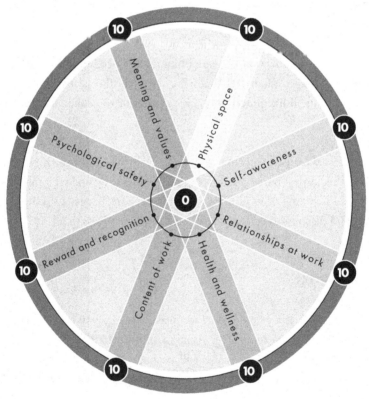

Draw your own Wheel of Work using the eight areas that we are going to explore in this book. Think about each of the following work areas in as much detail as possible:

1. Physical space: What impact the physical structure (lighting, air quality, sounds, temperatures, etc) of your workplace is having on your wellbeing and ability to do your work.
2. Self-awareness: How well you are able to make sense of and regulate your emotions and responses to the events that unfold at work.
3. Relationships at work: How socially connected and supported you feel at work.
4. Health and wellness: The way your physical, mental and emotional health and happiness are affected by the workplace, and affect your work.
5. Content of work: How satisfied and stimulated you are by what you're paid to spend your time on every day.
6. Reward and recognition: How noticed and appreciated you feel at work.
7. Psychological safety: How safe or unsafe you feel with the overt and covert values, ethos and expectations of the organisation and all members of it.
8. Meaning and values: The relationship between what is important to you and what is important to the organisation.

For each section, allocate a score between 0 (couldn't be less happy) and 10 (couldn't be happier) that illustrates your current level of satisfaction. Seeing the centre of the wheel as 0 and the outer rim as 10, rank your current level of satisfaction in each area of your work life by marking the appropriate place on the 'spoke' of the wheel, and then join the dots to create a wheel within the wheel.

NOW ASK YOURSELF:
○   If this were a wheel on your car, how smooth would your ride through work be?
○   To what degree do you feel that work is working for you in each of these eight areas?
○   Which work areas have you identified as being less than satisfactory?
○   Which areas are you satisfied with?
○   What is making you feel successful or unsuccessful in these areas?

If I were to have filled in a Wheel of Work for myself in the job I described, it would have looked like this:

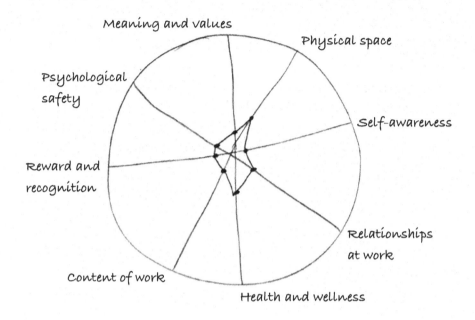

This wheel clearly shows how unhappy I was, how unfulfilling my work was, and how desperately slowly it was taking me forward in my life.

The Wheel of Work gives us an instant insight into where we are currently feeling that work is working for us, and where it isn't. It immediately shows us where we need to pay attention to make bad things better, or to keep good things good. The rounder our wheel, the smoother our work journey, and the larger the wheel, the swifter and greater the progress will be in our work life. Most people have a less than round Wheel of Work, which illustrates why our career journey can feel so bumpy and uncomfortable.

The next eight chapters of this book will explore each of the work areas in more detail, providing information and insights, and presenting tools and ideas to make each of the areas work better for you. Just as work is systemic in nature, each of the eight chapters is interrelated and interconnected.

As you are reading each chapter, think about how you can use what you are learning to improve the scores on your Wheel of Work and make your career ride a little smoother. How can you enhance what is already working for you, and address what isn't? What habits can you change or add to help you do this?

Habits

According to psychology professor Ian Walker, a habit is 'a behaviour that, through lots of repetition in a specific context, shifts from being triggered deliberately by your choices to being triggered automatically by the environment you're in'. So, what starts off a conscious decision to do some things in a certain way can quickly become a continued, unthinking practice: you brush your teeth when you emerge from the shower, you put the kettle on for a cup of tea when you go into the kitchen, you eat popcorn when you watch a movie, you scroll through socials when your phone is in your hand.

Many of our habits are good for us. Brushing and flossing our teeth every day, eating regular meals, greeting people we pass on our way... these are all good habits that help to keep us grounded and healthy by creating a self-supportive environment that provides predictability and continuity.

But many of our habits are not so good for us – especially the ones that emerged in response to a situation that no longer exists. Reading X (formerly known as Twitter) with my morning tea is a habit I got into during lockdown, when I had nowhere urgent to be and was fascinated (perhaps more than a little morbidly) with how Covid was evolving and showing up in the country and the world. Binge-watching series late into the night, wearing pyjamas (aka 'loungewear') all day, grazing on snacks rather than having healthy meals at mealtimes, and working odd hours are all examples of other not-such-great habits that many people got into in the dark days of the pandemic.

In and of themselves, there's nothing inherently wrong with any of these actions, but when they become routine, and when they take the place of more constructive and appropriate habits, they can start to negatively impact on our productivity, our peace of mind and our general health and wellness. Many of my clients, for example, still eat their lunch in front of their computers instead of using the time to exercise or get fresh air or socialise with colleagues, and most people I know struggle to stop themselves checking and responding to emails in the evenings and over weekends.

We need to consciously choose to get into the habit of doing things that are good for us, and for our work. As self-improvement coach James Clear puts it in his brilliant and accessible 2018 book, *Atomic Habits: Tiny Changes, Remarkable Results*, 'Habits are the compound interest of self-improvement.'

The challenge is to identify what you can do *every day* to improve your results. For sustainable results, we need to change the systems that cause the results – as Clear explains, we shouldn't be putting our attention on the end goal but should rather be thinking about the system/s we have in place to support the achievement of that goal, and identifying what we can do every day, in 'a system of continuous small improvements'. In his words, 'fix the inputs and the outputs will fix themselves'.

Ambivalence

Too often we set goals that we will never achieve: they are too ethereal or too ambitious or too demanding, or – worst of all – they are something that we don't feel passionate about but are agreeing to in order to keep someone else happy. Over and over again, I see people failing to meet goals that they are ambivalent about.

I have had more than a few clients who have berated themselves for not achieving a long-held goal – perhaps losing weight, or getting a promotion, or walking up the aisle. When we explore the goals in more depth and think through what they imagine their lives would look and feel like once that goal is achieved, we often uncover profound anxiety about how their lives may change. They may fear an expectation to be different if they are slimmer, or have to work longer hours and be away from their family more if they get promoted, or lose their independence and spontaneity if they get married…

Unless we are one hundred percent committed to achieving something – and by that I don't just mean committed to doing the work required but also committed to and convinced about the changes that will result when we achieve it – we are wasting our very precious time and energy while we go through the motions of pretending to work towards an outcome that we have mixed feelings about.

Even if we aren't ambivalent about the outcome, we need to set ourselves up for success by identifying goals that are achievable and realistic.

Introducing what I call 'tiny' habits – those that are tangible, implementable, nurturing and yours – will help you to set and attain goals that are important to you.

- **Tangible:** 'I will pack a healthy lunch every day' is tangible; 'I will eat more healthily' is not.
- **Implementable:** 'I will take healthy food to work' is implementable; 'I am never eating chocolate again' is not.
- **Nurturing:** Ensuring you have healthy, delicious snacks and lunches, including a sweet treat, to eat throughout the working day is nurturing; ignoring your hunger and thirst for eight hours is not.
- **Yours:** Giving yourself permission to take your lunch break wherever is relaxing and restorative to you is yours; eating lunch in front of your computer because you think it is expected of you is not.

I have been doing what I do for long enough to know that making grand gestures and setting grandiose goals does not help us to achieve the changes we want to make. It is only when my clients commit to small, strategic and sustainable steps that they reach their chosen destination.

If you are able to identify – and implement – 'tiny', tangible and maintainable habits to improve your experience in various aspects of your work, you will incrementally make it work better for you. As you work your way through this book, and the exercises and tasks I suggest you complete, I encourage you to think about 'tiny' habits that you can introduce in order to improve the system (and therefore your results) in each of your areas of discomfort or dissatisfaction.

What isn't (or wasn't) working at work

In order to make work work for us, we need to name and describe what is broken (or isn't working), so that we can identify and enact workable solutions. It helps to begin by airing all your grievances and cleaning out the festering wounds that work has inflicted on you, now and in the past.

○ Take out your notebook or a sheet of paper, as big as you need it to be, and write down all the things that (currently or in the past) upset/hurt/worried/angered/stressed you at work. Don't limit yourself to completing the task in one sitting — let it be a work in progress that you add to as you remember more things.

○ Use the eight areas in your Wheel of Work to help you to identify what about work doesn't (or didn't in the past) work for you. Capture anything and everything that you can think of that doesn't work for you at work. Don't worry about hurting anyone's feelings or getting into trouble; this is a private exercise for your eyes only. Let yourself go wild!

Here are a few of the many things I hated about my worst-ever jobs:
Horrible, buzzy, flickering fluorescent lighting
No fresh air or signs of natural life
A soulless workspace
Unpleasantly cold office temperature
No friends at work
Ugly, creepy picture on the wall
Boring and meaningless (to me) work
Not enough work to fill my long, unstimulating days
No space for taking initiative or being creative
A helicopter boss
No opportunity for career progress
Sunday night blues every night of the week

You may begin feeling a little overwhelmed as your list grows longer and longer – but do not despair. We can only work on what we know needs to be worked on.

Identifying all the things that are not working for you is bringing you one giant leap closer to making work work for you.

Each of the chapters that follow will look at some of the common discontents people experience at work – starting with the more practical, easier-to-address niggles of physical space, and then working our way through the more challenging and complicated issues.

Fixing what we can

A couple of jobs after leaving my job from hell, I was lucky enough to find something that was so fabulous I stayed there for over a decade. Still, despite it being a truly wonderful job, with interesting work and interested colleagues, I managed to find a few things that were less than perfect (I was the youngest member of staff, and being a youngest child too, I was apt to whine a bit).

Happily, I had a very wise boss who taught me one of the most powerful lessons I ever learned at and about work (and life). He told me that I was welcome to raise any problem or complaint I wanted to, as long as I offered a solution at the same time.

That one piece of advice and feedback moved me from being a serial complainer to becoming a stellar problem-solver, and it continues to stand me in good stead in all areas of my life. The discipline of thinking about ways to address every unhappiness helps me not only to actively improve my experience, but also to feel less helpless and more empowered. I know that the same will be true for you.

Obviously, not all problems have easy solutions. Some challenges are relatively easy to overcome or work around, while others are deeper and more complex. This book will give you ideas for some easy, quick wins, and also examine some of the more convoluted underlying issues that make work hard (boundaries, conflict and communication, meaning and values, and so on). I will share some of my most powerful tools (their power lies in their simplicity and ease of application) to help you to change your experience of work and the workplace for the better.

Let's start the journey of finding solutions to make your work work better for you!

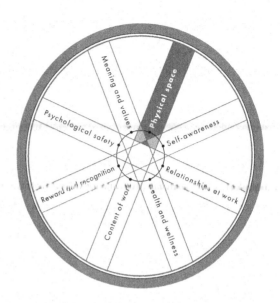

Physical space

Research is increasingly linking not just our quality of life to our physical environment, but also the quality of the work we do. Now, with a heightened awareness of burnout and the many environmental contributors to it, even more attention is being paid to the impact of our physical space on our health and wellness.

We spend up to a third of our time (and some people spend even more than that) working. It doesn't matter whether our workplace is in our home or in an office block, we must pay attention to making our workspaces as supportive and hospitable as we can.

Many years, and even more studies, have identified the most important elements necessary for productive, sustainable and happy workspaces. Along with access to safe and green outside areas, a work environment that is not too noisy or has too many intrusive sounds, and easy and safe access to clean toilets, there are four key requirements for productivity and conducive workspaces.

Air is, quite literally, the breath of life. We all know how much better and more energised we feel when we walk out of the building at the end of a working day. This isn't only because we're breathing a sigh of relief to be leaving work; it's also because, with that sigh, we're breathing in lovely, clean, fresh air, which is helping us to feel more relaxed and energised, and happier.

When the air that you're breathing is old, stale, tainted by chemicals and has been recycled through the building it inhabits a few thousand times, it doesn't do much to keep your lungs healthy and your head and thinking clear and creative. And stuffy spaces without fresh, circulating air increase the likelihood of our picking up germs and getting sick.

2. LIGHT AND LIGHTING

One of the things that used to freak me out the most about my job from hell was that I had no idea what to expect when I left the building. Would it be dark and rainy? Would the sun be shining? Would aliens have landed and taken over the streets of the city? Because the only window in the office was painted over, I literally had no frame of reference for what was going on outside.

Being able to track the organic progression of day into night and back into day is vital for our sleep and wake cycles. Yet an enormous percentage of the workforce, such as those who work in mega-office complexes, spend their days – often very long days – in environments with no natural light, or even exposure to the world outside. I'm convinced that restricting natural light has been a deliberate strategy on the part of many companies to keep their staff unaware of the passing of time – because if you don't realise that it's getting dark, you won't remember that you need to leave work and go home to have dinner with your family.

On top of that, the lighting in large buildings is often that very white, fluorescent lighting which flickers and hums and is a constant background irritation to our senses. It's harsh and unforgiving, and certainly contributed to many of the migraines I suffered in that environment.

Happily, there's a growing awareness and appreciation of the need for natural lighting, not only for our health and wellness, but also for our efficiency. The

International Labour Organization (ILO) has found that lighting in the workplace is important to prevent eye strain, headaches, fatigue, stress and accidents – and poor work quality and low productivity. A 2019 study showed that people who spent their days in natural light fell asleep more quickly, slept better and experienced less depression than people who spent their days in unnatural lighting, making them more effective at work and at home.

3. WATER/HYDRATION

When we get busy and stressed, we tend to forget about the most basic things that we need to be doing to look after ourselves. We run on adrenaline, switched off to the signals our bodies are sending us.

I start group sessions by encouraging participants to check in with their bodies by asking themselves what they're feeling and why they're feeling that way. Almost always, particularly if the session is towards the end of the day, at least one person will realise that they have a headache because they haven't had enough or, often, any water to drink the whole day.

The Human Performance Laboratory at the University of Connecticut identified that dehydration leads to reduced energy levels, impaired cognitive performance and a weakened immune system – all of which add up to reduced productivity and increased unhappiness in the workplace. It's hard to be cheerful and creative when you have a pounding headache – as anyone who's had to suffer through a day at work with a hangover will tell you.

Water coolers aren't only a good place to catch up with colleagues and discuss the latest scandal; they're an important source of hydration and the productivity that comes with it.

If you're worried that drinking a lot will mean you need to visit the bathroom more often, do not despair: walking and movement are also important elements of a healthy and productive working day.

4. MOVEMENT

Digital connectivity – and all that comes with it, such as smartphones and their apps, email, intra-office mail and the like – is a wonderful tool that has made a major and important contribution, and we're very grateful to it for the countless enhancements it has brought to our professional lives.

That said, our reliance on gadgets and electronics means that we're less likely to get up and walk over to ask a colleague a question. Remote communication not only impacts on the relationship-building and other informal processes that are so valuable in any workplace, but also means that many of us sit still for too many hours on end. Being sedentary has become such a problem that there is now a whole 'sitting is the new smoking' movement, which asserts that sitting is as dangerous to us as – if not more so than – smoking. The Heart Foundation of America has found that extended periods of sitting increase the risk of diabetes, heart attacks and strokes. This is because when we sit for too long, our blood flow slows down, which allows fats to build up, leading to heart disease, blood clots and insulin resistance.

And, once again, it isn't just a health issue but also one of productivity and effectiveness: the more we move, the more oxygen goes to our brain, and the more creative and productive we become.

Face your space

The thing about our physical environment is that the longer we spend in it, the less aware we become of its impact on us. We become inured to it and, much like the proverbial frog in the slowly heating-up pot of water, we tend to pay less and less attention to the irritations and discomforts we endure, until we stop noticing them altogether.

When we first arrive in a new place, we're very aware of what it looks and feels like – we hear every car driving past, we notice the buzz of the fluorescent lights, we smell the scent (or stench, depending on how sensitive we are) of the furniture polish… But as we become habituated, we may stop noticing the finer details. The environmental discomfort fades into the background as the pressure of the work takes centre stage.

Nonetheless, whether we're noticing it or not, our physical environment continues to influence our health, wellness and productivity. So, even if spatial factors are no longer uppermost in your mind, you may still be affected by them un- or sub-consciously.

Do a thorough audit of your physical environment. How does the space you work in fit you – and how do you fit into the space? What about your physical environment at work makes you happy? What about it makes you unhappy?

Ask yourself:
○ How the space looks. Does it look appealing to you? Is it too light or too dark? Do the psychedelic carpets give you a headache? Can you see outside?
○ How the space feels. Is the ambient temperature too hot or too cold or just right? Do you have not enough, too much or just the right amount of personal space? Can you move around easily or do you feel hemmed in?
○ How the space smells. Are there any smells that especially delight or revolt you? Is the air you are breathing fresh and refreshing, or not so much?
○ How the space sounds. Is it too noisy, too quiet or just right? Are the sounds (or the silence) helpful or distracting?
○ How you feel when you leave the space. Do you notice a change in your body and/or your mood when you leave the space?

Because we're not robots, we're affected by sounds, smells, sights, temperatures and light. Our senses are triggered by the place we're in and what we're exposed to there.

Here are some suggestions for how to make your physical space feel more comfortable:

1. AIR QUALITY

Open as many windows as possible, as widely as you can. If you work in a building that has air-conditioning and no opening windows, try to ensure that you're breathing in fresh air at least every couple of hours for a few minutes. Think like a smoker – ironically, the people who go outside to smoke are probably getting more fresh, clean air than those who stay at their desks all day. Optimally, too, you should be finding an outside space to have your lunch in.

19

When you hit the after-lunch slump or are struggling to find the words to complete a report, rather than reaching for another cup of coffee, try going outside for some fresh air and a change of scenery. You'll be amazed how quickly your creative juices will start flowing out there.

2. LIGHT AND LIGHTING

I picked up a wonderful lighting hack when I was on sabbatical in Canada, where it's light for an average of just seven hours a day in mid-winter, and the locals have learned a thing or two about enduring long, dark winters with unavoidable artificial lighting. Most people have a table lamp on their desks; and not a harsh, bright lamp, but one with a gentle light that softens the intense ambient lighting and makes everything feel cosier and less severe. I use my desk lamp to brighten up a grey day and to provide a warm light on the evenings that I work.

3. WATER/HYDRATION

It can be difficult to remember to drink enough – particularly when it's an effort to get to the kitchen or water cooler. We have to ensure that it's as easy as possible to get enough water into us.

If your workplace doesn't have a water cooler – or even if it does – it's a good idea to work out your own way of hydrating yourself. Get a water bottle that you can carry around with you. Put a jug of lemon-enhanced water on your desk. Bring some herbal teas to work for when you need a warm drink. While pure, fresh water is best for hydration, any non-alcoholic liquid drink will do the trick (just go easy on the sugar, which will cancel out the benefits of the liquid intake).

Fresh fruit and veggies are also a good way to get additional hydration into your body and your brain.

4. MOVEMENT

Rather than picking up your phone to ask a colleague a question, walk to their office and have a chat to them in person. Set a timer to remind yourself to get up and move every hour. Take the stairs instead of the lift, even if you start by walking down the stairs and catching the lift back up.

Walk more – go for a walk at lunch time, and set up 'walking meetings' with amenable colleagues. You'll be amazed at how much more creative and insightful you'll become when you tackle a problem while walking.

Instead of checking your social media whenever your brain needs a break, stand up and stretch behind your desk. Better still, check your social media *while* standing and stretching.

Remove it or improve it

If I had thought about *removing or improving* what I could when working at the job from hell, I would have been able to make my working life so much more pleasant, and I wouldn't have been nearly as sick and unhappy as I was for those months of misery. These are some of the things that I could have done to remove or improve my worries.

Problem	Remove it?	Improve it...
Headache-inducing lighting	Turn off overhead lights if possible	Bring in a table lamp with a warm, low-wattage bulb to soften the lighting
Soulless workspace		Put a pretty scarf over my chair; get a mug that makes me happy to have my tea from
Ugly picture on the wall	Take it down and hide it in the cupboard	Replace it with a picture that makes me happy – or leave the wall bare
No fresh air		Go outside as often as possible (for tea and lunch breaks)
No signs of natural life		Put pot plants and fresh flowers (even if picked from a garden on the way to work) and a bowl of fresh fruit on my desk
Arctic temperatures		Have scarves and wraps to hand; bring in a small heater

Now it's your turn to identify what, where and how you can remove and/or improve some of the things that are making you unhappy at work.

You should have a pretty comprehensive list of complaints from the last task you completed (see page 19), among which will be issues related to your physical workspace. Now you're going to think of ways that you can enhance the bits that make you happy, and ways that you can address the bits that make you unhappy.

Using a highlighter or brightly coloured pen, circle all the things on your list that are mostly simple and straightforward – the things related to your physical space that you can easily remove or improve. Examine each item in turn and ask, can I remove this or can I improve it? If you can remove it, then do so – get rid of it! If that isn't possible, think about how you can improve it.

For instance, if your very own window makes you happy, you could enhance it by making sure that it's always clean, and/or you could put some of your own pot plants on the windowsill or hang some wind chimes from the frame. If, however, the lack of a window makes you unhappy, you could think about ways that you can see outside; maybe you could put up a poster of an outside scene on your wall or find a communal area that has a window where you can take your tea and lunch breaks. Or you could actually go outside instead of just missing looking outside.

Remember to pay particular attention to seeing how you can ensure as much natural light, fresh air, movement and hydration as possible.

SIMPLE IS OFTEN BEST

It may all sound too good to be true, but the most effective tools and approaches are usually the simplest ones.

Noah was sent for coaching because he had lost his spark and his boss was worried that he was in a downward spiral, not just professionally but also physically and emotionally. It turned out that, for a variety of very real and distressing reasons – many of them financial – he was eating badly, drinking too much alcohol and not enough water, exercising not at all, and sleeping poorly. It was no wonder his work was suffering.

We established that he needed to address his health before we could do anything else. Because Noah lived a couple of kilometres from work, he decided that he would start walking to and from work, which would give him some exercise in the fresh air while saving money on petrol. Instead of buying fried takeaways every lunch time, he packed a healthy lunch for himself while he was making his children's school lunches, saving him money and ensuring healthier eating. He got a large water bottle to carry around with him, which helped him to drink at least a litre of water every day at work.

In this way, he introduced three 'tiny' habits: walking to work, packing a healthy lunch and drinking enough water. By making those changes, Noah lost weight, saved money, slept better, and gained energy and enthusiasm which he put into his family and his work.

Within a few weeks, Noah was back to being the employee (and husband and father) that everyone recognised and valued. I can still see the light and lightness returning to him, all these years later.

Simple isn't always easy – it does require effort and commitment – but it is almost always best.

Although it may seem that addressing your working environment is akin to putting a band-aid on a severed artery, you'll be amazed at how huge an impact improving your physical space has on your emotional wellbeing. First, you'll feel more capable and empowered, and less helpless and hopeless. And, second, you'll notice that as your external environment becomes a nicer to place to be, so will your internal environment. It's a bit like noticing how much more powerful and faster your car becomes after you've taken it to be washed!

Can you think of two or three 'tiny' habits that will help you to improve your level of satisfaction in this area and allow your Wheel of Work to give you a smoother ride?

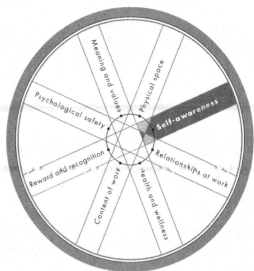

Self-awareness and self-management

We're often so caught up in feeling that things happen to us at work that we forget to pay attention to the role we play and how we contribute to what happens at work. Every relationship, every interaction and every disagreement is a sum of its individual parts, and if we're unaware of the part we're playing, those sums can get pretty complicated and difficult to solve.

When we become more self-aware, we gain insight into our actions and reactions, and increase the probability of a harmonious environment where work works for us.

How we get in our own way

A couple of years ago I ran a session for a group of young entrepreneurs who were part of a start-up incubator. I presented ideas and tools for self-care, getting out of your own way, and reaching your full potential. I was asked to speak to the entrepreneurs because their head mentor, who had worked with me in the past, recognised that they all had at least some 'adult child' characteristics – many of the positive ones that ensured their entrepreneurial strengths but also a few of the more challenging ones that were getting in the way of their success.

THE CHARACTERISTICS OF ADULT CHILDREN

In the 1980s, psychologist Janet Woititz observed that many of her patients who had grown up with alcoholic parent/s had very similar habits and characteristics. She came up with the term 'adult children of alcoholics' to acknowledge the range of behaviours and traits that are common to people who grew up in homes with addiction.

In her 1983 book, *Adult Children of Alcoholics (& Other Dysfunctional Families)*, Dr Woititz identified 13 characteristics of adult children. According to her, adult children:
1. guess at what normal behaviour is;
2. have difficulty following a project through from beginning to end;
3. lie when it would be just as easy to tell the truth;
4. judge themselves without mercy;
5. have difficulty having fun;
6. take themselves very seriously;
7. have difficulty with intimate relationships;
8. overreact to changes over which they have no control;
9. constantly seek approval and affirmation;
10. usually feel that they are different from other people;
11. are super-responsible or super-irresponsible;
12. are extremely loyal, even in the face of evidence that the loyalty is undeserved;
13. are impulsive.

I have worked with numerous clients who have at least some of the characteristics of adult children, even if they didn't have a parent who was an alcoholic or an addict, so I have broadened the meaning and definition of an 'adult child' to include anyone who grew up in an environment that was inconsistent or unpredictable in some way or for some time – which is a whole lot of us.

There are a range of possible reasons for the inconsistency and unpredictibility so many adults experienced as children. These include addiction (such as alcohol, drugs or gambling, in either parents or siblings), financial stresses, parents who are separated or divorced or not present at all, having a special-needs sibling where all the parents' attention was on the sibling, parent or parents with chronic illnesses, including depression or any kind of physical or mental illness, or moving often.

Even for those people who had a very stable, nuclear family and a childhood with no surprises, the broader environment also has a role to play in adult child characteristics. Even if our family environment is stable and predictable, our macro environment often isn't. Certainly, for those of us who grew up in South Africa, our macro environment has never been stable or predictable.

It is essential to recognise that there are countless positives to being an adult child – many of which make us who we are as South Africans. We are reliable, resourceful, resilient, responsible and very good in a crisis. We are excellent and creative problem solvers. We are intuitive and empathetic. We are irrepressible and are almost always able to 'make a plan'. We add enormous value to any team or organisation.

And we are generally quite independent, which means that we don't need to be babysat when we are at work – and/but we don't like to be micromanaged. This is why so many adult children work for themselves; we don't always do very well with being told what to do.

In the session for the entrepreneurs, I started off by describing my work with adult children and asserting my belief that most of us have at least some of the characteristics that are common to those of us who grew up in environments that were chaotic in some way or another. Most of the young men in the room nodded kindly but I could tell they were being polite and didn't really see how this information was in any way relevant to them and their start-up companies.

As I started to go into more detail about the characteristics and how they manifest in our lives, however, the entrepreneurs began to sit up and pay a bit more attention. And as I talked about how adapting to looking out for ourselves, protecting ourselves from shame and disappointment, and learning how to make do with whatever we have all impact on our ability to work and succeed, the room lit up with all the lightbulbs that were going off in their minds. The statements that got the most rueful smiles and headshakes were 'Adult children struggle to ask for help and to say "no"', 'We lie when it is just as easy to tell the truth' and 'We have difficulty following projects through from beginning to end'.

When I described how, as a self-employed adult child, I used to take on much too much work (including work that I had no interest in and sometimes no affinity for) and never contemplated getting help in the form of assistance or feedback – ultimately resulting in the cardinal sin of over-promising and under-delivering – I could see the relief of recognition in all their faces. The feeling of 'I'm not the only one' is hugely liberating and empowering to people who have borne a load of unconscious and unhelpful beliefs and behaviours their whole lives.

Many of us have learned to protect ourselves by pretending to be coping when we aren't, by not admitting when we could do with some guidance, and by asserting that we can do something that we can't. We have set ourselves up for disappointment at best and failure at worst – and whole lot of energy-sapping anxiety along the way. Lying when it is just as easy to tell the truth may feel like the right thing to do in the moment, but it creates a lot of angst and unhappiness in the future.

To illustrate how difficult we can make our lives when we lie instead of telling the truth, I related the story of one of my clients, Jake.

Jake was so desperate for a promotion and the salary increase that came with it that he assured his manager that he would be able to produce a lengthy report which included a complex spreadsheet by the following week. So anxious was he not to appear unprofessional and inept that he agreed to do something that he had no experience in (having never done a spreadsheet before) and for which he was never going to meet the time requirement.

When it became clear that Jake had got himself into a whole lot of trouble, he scheduled a quick-coaching session with me to figure out what he could do to salvage the situation. Once he had calmed down and was able to see things from the perspective of the competent grownup professional he was, rather than the frightened child he had been feeling like, Jake decided that he needed to go back to his manager and explain that in order to deliver the kind of report that was expected of him, he needed more time to work on it. He also admitted that he would greatly benefit from working with someone who excelled at spreadsheets and could give him the kind of feedback and input he needed.

Jake's manager was so impressed that Jake had taken proactive steps to avert the late delivery of a substandard report, he happily granted Jake's requests, and commended him for his honesty and professionalism. Jake not only dodged disaster but gained the respect of his manager and was able to bring his anxiety levels down from astronomic to acceptable.

Jake's story shows that it doesn't have to be a big lie to have potentially big consequences, and when I related it to the young men in the incubator session they looked at each other, had a chuckle and all – every one of them – shared stories of how they, too, had been less than honest, had not said 'no', or had not asked for help (or a combination of the three) in the past, and how it had added to their stress and anxiety, which had in turn negatively impacted on their ability to get the recognition and support they desperately wanted and needed.

I closed the session by reminding them that not all of the common characteristics of adult children are negative; many are positive and constructive. From being extremely sceptical about the idea of being adult children who unknowingly were getting in their own way of success, the entrepreneurs were all able to identify with some of these positive characteristics. They were able to mindfully choose which traits – such as their creativity and irrepressibleness – to build on, and which ones to stop being held hostage by.

HOW THE 'ADULT CHILDREN' CHARACTERISTICS IMPACT OUR WORK

The characteristics of adult children show up in different combinations and intensities for everyone, but there are recognisable patterns in how some of them can make work difficult.

As the story I told the start-up entrepreneurs shows, one of the most common ways we trip ourselves up at work (and everywhere else) is by 'lying when it is just as easy to tell the truth'. These are not the kinds of lies that dodgy politicians tell; they're not malevolent or malicious lies. The kinds of lies we tell are designed to save face, to protect us from harm or humiliation. So we say 'I'm fine' when we're clearly not coping, or 'Oh yes, I can do that' when actually we have no idea how to even start, or 'I don't need help' when we most certainly do.

Many people resist asking for help either because they don't want to show weakness, appear vulnerable or because their experience of asking for help has not ended well – they might have asked for help in the past and not received it, or been ridiculed or made to feel useless or incompetent.

But mostly I think it doesn't even occur to us to ask for help.

Often, when my clients are telling me about something they're struggling with, and I say, 'Could you ask somebody for help with that?', they look at me as if I've just spoken some kind of biblical truth that they'd never even considered. We've been so conditioned by ourselves and by our environments to just get on with things and to make things happen for ourselves that help doesn't feel like an option.

Struggling to ask for help is one of the reasons so many of us 'have difficulty following projects through from beginning to end'. We may start a project with great enthusiasm, but as soon as it gets a bit tricky or something else more interesting comes along, we start losing steam. And rather than asking for help to make it less difficult or more interesting, we often don't finish what we start. This is not necessarily a problem when it relates to not finishing the blanket you started to crochet, but it is unhelpful when it means abandoning a work project or a training programme that is important for a promotion or an increase.

'Overreacting to changes over which we have no control' is another characteristic that can make work challenging. Change is always hard – even when we choose it, but especially when we don't. Getting that promotion we wanted and worked towards is exciting and affirming – and it's also difficult to adapt to the new role, the different expectations and the changed relationships with colleagues. But when a trusted colleague resigns and leaves the organisation, or when we're assigned to a new team without being consulted, it's even more difficult to adapt to the strangeness of the changed environment.

Anything that makes us feel like we don't have any agency can make life feel very scary for us. Interestingly, adult children are generally very good in a crisis, and are able to adapt to and manage big things, so after a few days of discomfort, we generally settle in well to our new or changed environment and make the most of the relationships and work we are now exposed to.

At a more micro level, though, when a deadline is shifted or a deliverable changed, it can be very unsettling and if, as many of us tend to do, we take it personally and feel victimised by the changes, it can send us into a flat spin of worrying about whether what we deliver will be good enough.

Worrying about not being good enough or not doing well enough leads into another characteristic of adult children, which is that of 'judging ourselves without mercy'. We can be extremely hard on ourselves, especially in the workplace. This merciless judging contributes to our struggles with saying 'no', asking for help, and telling the truth. Even though we want to do everything brilliantly and perfectly, we can't allow ourselves to seek the help we need to achieve this perfection.

'Constantly seeking approval and affirmation' goes along with judging ourselves without mercy. We want to have feedback, we want people to tell us how well we're doing, and we want to be noticed and appreciated and recognised for the work we do. The difficulty is that, because of judging ourselves so harshly, we often don't trust the affirmation when it comes; we think people are just being nice to us because they feel sorry for us – and that makes us push ourselves even harder (without help), which in turn makes us vulnerable to becoming overwhelmed and burned out.

Because we judge ourselves so harshly and take ourselves very seriously, it can be hard for us to relax and have fun, especially in the workplace where we often feel as though we need to be on our very best behaviour. So it can be difficult to make friends at work and join in with work extramurals, leaving us feeling lonely and isolated, and making asking for help seem even less of an option.

Lastly, as Woititz pointed out, many adult children are extremely loyal, even in the face of clear evidence that the loyalty is undeserved. This makes us stay in jobs that we hate – often because we're worried about leaving people behind when we move on. A number of my clients struggle with the idea of leaving their colleagues who have come to feel like family; they feel it would be disloyal for them to move on to greener pastures and leave behind people who are important to them.

Sometimes a few of the adult child characteristics, which are all the more powerful and impactful because we're acting on them largely unconsciously, come together in a perfect storm of anxiety, resentment and burnout that gets in the way of our success and career sustainability.

Matthew signed up for coaching because he had a sense that he was getting in the way of taking his small business to the next level and making it profitable. As he learned about the adult child characteristics, Matthew realised that his ability to problem solve and go the extra mile for his many somewhat demanding clients ensured that his business was so busy that he had a waiting list for new clients. Unfortunately, however, he wasn't covering his costs.

He recognised that he had been judging himself and his work mercilessly and, because he always feared that he wasn't doing a good enough job, he had been drastically undercharging and running himself ragged, leading him to the cusp of burnout.

Happily, he was able to see what he was doing and how he was getting in his own way and was able to address his impostor syndrome (see page 49), put up some boundaries, increase his rates, and say no to work that wasn't working for him.

Once he had made these changes, a core set of clients became even more appreciative of his work and he was able to serve fewer clients, doing less work and making more money.

Matthew's experience shows that when we are aware of the behaviours that we have unintentionally picked up, and mindfully work with them and the countless positive characteristics of being an adult child – our resourcefulness, creativity, compassion, empathy, ability to adapt, and so many more – we can turn these characteristics into assets and achieve the levels of satisfaction and success we are worthy of.

Do you recognise any of the adult child traits in yourself? Using your Wheel of Work (see page 8) as a prompt, explore each area of work in relation to the adult child information.

Ask yourself:
○ Have any of the adult child characteristics got in the way of your making work work for you? If so, how?
○ How have some of the positive aspects – the resilience, the resourcefulness, the creativity, the being good in a crisis, the empathy – helped you to succeed?
○ What 'tiny' habit can you introduce to make the most of your strengths and/or limit the impact of the challenges?

TELLING OURSELVES THE TRUTH

Of all of the characteristics of adult children, the one that has perhaps the greatest impact on our lives and our work is the propensity to hide from the truth.

Sometimes we bite back the truth because we're too polite, or because we don't want to hurt someone's feelings. And sometimes we're less than truthful about our abilities because we don't want to get into trouble, or lose a job, or let anyone down.

The lies we tell are almost always untruths we tell ourselves, let alone anyone else. We get ourselves into all sorts of pickles when we aren't honest about how we're feeling or what we're needing – for example, when a colleague asks for help and we leap immediately to assist, rather than being open about the fact that we have our own deadline to meet; or when a supervisor allocates us a task and, like Jake, we're too anxious or fearful to admit that we aren't sure how to go about doing it; or when a client asks us to deliver something by a certain time and date and we aren't confident enough to say that we need more time to do a good job.

It doesn't matter whether it's concern for someone else's feelings or concern for our own reputation, not being honest about what we can and can't do, or do and don't want to manage, is a sure-fire way to find ourselves taking on tasks that expose us to leaky boundaries and resentment, and from there down the rocky road to burnout.

What lies — big or small — have you been telling yourself and others about your work? Jot down all the many and varied lies you have told up to this point (remembering that sometimes we lie by omission). These might include saying you have capacity for a new project when you're already overwhelmed, agreeing to a task that you don't really have the skills to manage, pretending to love rugby because you know your boss does, or turning a blind eye (and closed lips) to workplace behaviour that offends you. Now ask yourself:

○   Why did you tell those lies? Was it to protect yourself? Was it to protect someone else — and their feelings?
○   What was or is the consequence of the lie/s? Did it end well for you and everyone else?
○   Is there a way that you can revisit the lie/s and tell the truth, releasing yourself from unnecessary stress and anxiety?

There are always going to be some lies that we choose to tell in order to grease the social wheels – pretending to be enthusiastic about rugby when you aren't, for instance. These untruths aren't harmful in any way (other than perhaps having to talk more about rugby than you may choose to!) and don't do any damage. The lies that we need to avoid are the stories we tell without thinking through the consequences – stories that may lead us deeper and deeper into trouble and anxiety.

We can only be honest with others when we're telling ourselves the truth. And we can only be honest with ourselves when we create the time and space to do so. Saying 'let me think about it and come back to you in a few minutes' is an effective way to give yourself the opportunity to realistically assess if you have the capacity to do something that has been asked of you.

Communication

One of the ways that we trip ourselves up at work is by not speaking up and communicating our needs and wants, and by not managing conflict constructively or by avoiding it completely. When we don't feel equipped to express ourselves calmly and rationally, we can't allow ourselves to ask for help, to say 'no', to set and maintain good boundaries or to share ideas in a powerful way. Not feeling heard, not feeling understood and not feeling able to express ourselves properly all contribute to workplace alienation and discontent.

Jane came to me for coaching because she needed help managing her emotions and communicating clearly and competently. She was liable to veer between flying off the handle when asked to do something she didn't want to do, feeling overly responsible for her peers and exhausting herself by doing much of their work for them, and feeling abject terror that her boss was going to reprimand her for not doing her job well enough. It was exhausting for her and frustrating for everyone around her.

Through our conversations, we were able to identify that for most of her time in the office, Jane felt like a grumpy, recalcitrant toddler (usually when she was given instructions), an exhausted and over-involved mother responsible for looking after others, or a terrified child waiting to get into trouble for failing an assignment. Her periods of feeling calm, competent and in charge were few and far between. It was no wonder she was frazzled and having fantasies of running away to join the circus.

Jane also explained that she had loads of ideas that she knew would benefit the company but that she didn't ever feel confident enough to share them because she was convinced – despite no evidence to support this – that she would be ridiculed and humiliated when she spoke.

It was a classic case of slipping out of her 'Adult' ego state, and falling into the 'Child' or 'Parent' states instead. I let her into the secret of transactional analysis, taught her my magic trick for calm, rational, assertive communication, and sent her on her way.

She emailed me a few weeks after our last session to tell me that she had just had a performance review, and that her manager and peers all reported being blown away by the change in her demeanour at work, her ability to engage positively with other staff members, and her new gift of managing conflict constructively.

Transactional analysis is a model that helps us understand how we communicate, how we interact and how we respond in interactions. German psychiatrist Eric Berne, the 'father of transactional analysis', was interested in deepening our understanding of communication, and particularly the interactions – or 'transactions', as he called them – that take place between people.

Berne identified that all of us – every single one of us, no matter how young or old – has three ego states, or states of being (the way we are feeling and behaving): Parent, Adult and Child.

When we're in our Parent ego state, we're either feeling and being judgemental or controlling (the 'critical Parent'), or we're feeling and being very concerned and caring (the 'nurturing Parent'). It's easy to think that we're only in our Parent state when we're talking to our children, but we can get into Parent state when we're talking to peers, elders and superiors. It's an emotional response rather than a relational one.

The critical Parent part of us is activated when we're feeling very obviously critical or controlling; pointing our finger, judging, telling people what to do or belittling them: Why can't you pick your socks up off the floor? Why do you leave everything to the last minute? Why didn't you tell me you were going to be late to work today?

When we're in our nurturing Parent state, we're feeling and acting very kindly and lovingly; we want to help and make things better for the other person. Jane operated from her nurturing Parent state whenever she felt sorry for a colleague and took over their work for them.

The Child ego state has three masks: the 'natural' or 'free Child', the 'frightened Child' and the 'rebellious Child'. When we're in the state of natural or free Child, we're able to feel carefree, like we don't have any responsibilities, with not a worry in the world. We often get into this state when we're playing with actual children or when we're with our friends, kicking back and relaxing, and with no sense of needing to do anything or look after anything.

When we're in the frightened Child state, we're very scared of being hurt (either physically or emotionally), being rejected, or being shamed or made to feel humiliated. When Jane was too scared to speak up in a meeting, or was waiting for feedback from her boss, she was in her frightened Child state, anxious and scared that she was going to be told that she wasn't good enough. When she was told to do something that she didn't want or feel able to do, she would slip into her rebellious Child state and have an angry outburst, just like a toddler who has a temper tantrum when things don't go their way.

When we're in our Adult ego state, we're calm and rational. We feel empowered and we don't react impulsively, but respond mindfully and appropriately to the situation we find ourselves in. Jane hadn't been spending much time in her Adult state until she learned to tune into her physical and emotional feelings, and actively shift herself out of her Parent or Child state and into her Adult state.

It's the critical Parent part of us that makes us judge ourselves without mercy; and it's the frightened Child that seeks approval and affirmation, has difficulty following projects through from beginning to end, and struggles to say 'no' and ask for help. It's the Adult part of us that is competent and accomplished, and guides us to success.

Because of how organisations – even the smallest – are set up, the kinds of interactions that transactional analysis describes play out regularly; and because our ego states aren't fixed, we can shift from one to another in a second, depending on the interaction we're having in that moment. Bosses, managers, supervisors – anyone in a 'higher up' position – assume or are assigned the role of 'parents', while subordinates and people we manage are the 'children', and our colleagues and peers are like our siblings, the other 'children' in the house. Is it any wonder that so many of us are unconsciously repeating the trials and tribulations we experienced in our childhood homes?

The intriguing and enlightening thing about this model is that each of our ego states is interacting unconsciously and automatically with other people's ego states. According to Berne, we're all communicating with each other's ego states all the time, and the words we're using are not nearly as powerful as the way we're feeling when we use those words. It's the way we're feeling – the ego state that we're in – when we're communicating, that people are responding to.

What Jane was unaware of was this clear, albeit unconscious, interaction that plays out between the ego states of people who are interacting with each other. So the more anxious and frightened of not being good enough she felt, the more critical and judgemental her manager became, which in turn made Jane feel even more anxious and unworthy. And the sulkier and more uncooperative she felt, the bossier and more critical her boss would become. And the more she nurtured and tried to save her colleagues, the more they eased into allowing her to do their work for them.

Jane – like the rest of us – had been largely unaware of the role she was playing in her own uncomfortable and unconstructive interactions. As soon as she learned about and was able to recognise her ego states, she consciously chose to respond from her Adult state, rather than from her Child or Parent states. As a result, almost immediately all her relationships, at work and outside of work, improved dramatically. Jane – and everyone around her – experienced less anger, less anxiety and less drama, and more peace and calm.

The transactions that Berne described are taking place in offices, homes and traffic jams all over the world – we all slip out of our Adult state and into our Parent and Child states regularly and frequently. It's very easy to slip into our Parent or Child state in our communications, particularly when we're tired, anxious or stressed. It's perfectly normal. The problem is that the less conscious we are in our transactions, the more likely they are to be, or become, fraught and conflictual.

If we are to reach a state of neutral calm, where we can speak to be heard and listen to understand, where we can make work work for us, we need to consciously communicate and transact from our Adult ego state as often as possible. But in order to pull this off, we need to be very present and very mindful.

The magic trick I teach my clients to help them do this is to identify an Adult role model: someone who exemplifies all the qualities they most want to exhibit – someone who is calm, rational, empowered and measured in their responses. You could almost say your Adult role model is the person you aspire to be as the very best version of yourself. They can be real or imagined, living or dead, but you must not know them too well; in other words, no family members, best friends or anyone else you're very familiar with. Oprah, Nelson Mandela, Martin Luther

King, religious leaders, teachers from childhood, and characters from books or movies are all examples of the role models I have heard identified.

Jane chose a teacher she had admired in high school, and every time she caught herself feeling anxious or scared (in her frightened Child state), sulky and uncooperative (rebellious Child), or as though she had to swoop in save someone from themselves (nurturing Parent), she asked herself, 'What would Mrs Brown do in this situation?' Just asking that question created a pause and allowed her to think about a suitable and constructive response, rather than reacting impulsively and habitually.

As soon as we give ourselves the space to objectively view the situations we find ourselves in, and to imagine how the best and most mature and empowered version of ourselves would respond, we create the conditions for calm, constructive and productive Adult interactions.

What do you do when you get a late-night email, or yet another friend or colleague arrives at your door to have a chat while you're chasing a deadline, or you want to ask for a raise in salary or in the temperature of the office?

Rather than reacting from your Parent or Child ego states, imagine what your Adult role model would say and how they would say it, and go ahead and say it. You'll be amazed at how easy and effective it is to find solutions to problems when you use this strategy.

In order to help you do this proactively, ask yourself:
o   Who are the people at work who bring out your critical/nurturing Parent or frightened/ rebellious Child states?
o   What kinds of tasks or activities cause you to move out of your Adult ego state?
o   How your role model (your Mrs Brown) would respond to these people and tasks?
o   What new 'tiny' habit would help to make your transactions more appropriate and professional?

How can you help yourself to stay in your Adult ego state as much as possible (for example, pause before reacting, take time to write a considered and constructive response to emails, imagine you are your role model as you sit down at your desk every day...)?

It might be helpful to revisit your 'not working at work' list you drew up on page 12, and ask your

Adult role model how they would address the items on it.

Think back on three (or more) times that you've been able to succeed and feel good about yourself at work. What ego state do you think you accessed when you were busy with that task or project? My guess is it was your Adult! And even if you started in your Parent or Child state, you probably managed to shift into Adult at some stage, which is what got you to the point of success.

We aren't always aware of it, but the way we're feeling has a profound impact on the way we behave and how we interact with other people. Understanding our ego states and how they interact with the people around us is a game-changer – not just in terms of how we communicate and manage conflict with others, but also in relation to our self-talk and how we conduct ourselves.

How we take our wounds to work

Amir had been coming for coaching on and off for years, first for support as he recovered from extreme burnout, and then for career-related issues.

During our first few sessions, we'd established that Amir was burned out to a crisp, largely due to his propensity to push himself too far and too hard in the quest to gain the approval and affirmation of his manager. Amir was able to make the link between his less-than-idyllic childhood with a hypercritical father who was scathing and belittling most of the time, and the environment in which he found himself at work.

We'd dealt with the burnout, and he'd set up and maintained an excellent self-care regimen. When Amir returned a few years later it was because he was finding work so stressful that he was worried he was going to burn out again. It wasn't everything about work, however; it was only his boss that he was finding so upsetting and destabilising. 'She's just like my father! Nothing I do is good enough. If I do manage to meet her ridiculously high standards of approval, she never acknowledges my effort, always finds something to complain about and tells me I should do better,' he told me.

Whenever a client says that someone in their life is 'just like my mother/father', I sit up and take notice because it's almost always a clue to understanding not just the responses of my clients to the people who remind them of their parent/s, but also the patterns and choices they have made over many years.

We start learning by watching, and as we develop, we begin to learn through experience – we learn by doing. In other words, we learn how to be in the world by watching and interacting with the grownups. As we grow up and widen the scope of our social net, we add more relationships to our experience: relatives, friends, romantic partners, bosses… Our experiences of relationships in our childhood add up and contribute to how we experience relationships – with lovers, friends, family members, bosses or colleagues – as adults.

Our early relationships with our parents, caregivers and family were an experience of love and acceptance – or, sadly, sometimes the lack thereof. These early relationships are almost always the foundation for the relationships we have in later life. If we felt loved and accepted, noticed and appreciated in our early relationships, we will expect and allow those same feelings in our grownup relationships. If our early interactions were not so easy or affirming, we may find it hard to be in easy and affirming relationships as adults. And if our early relationships were fraught and filled with drama and disappointment, well… we all know how that will probably turn out.

When we have a deep or core wound, we tend to be attracted to a partner who activates that wound (for example, if we experienced disapproval as a child, we may unconsciously find partners who are difficult to please). This is pretty well understood in our romantic lives, but we see it playing out in the workplace as well.

Amir had found himself working for a woman who he felt was just as impossible to please or to get any acknowledgement from as his father had been. When I asked him if this was his first boss who had been like this, he realised that there was a pattern in his having bosses who were as critical and hard to please as his current one. Amir himself was the common denominator: he was unconsciously finding (or creating) situations that provided him with the opportunity to get right with his boss what he couldn't with his dad.

41

The big question is, what role was Amir playing in the dynamic between him and his boss? He thought about it at length and started to pay attention to his interactions with his boss. At the end of every day, he wrote in his journal to try and make sense of the dynamic that had developed between the two of them. Every evening he wrote about the following:

- *What he had interacted with the boss about that day.*
- *How he had felt at the beginning, middle and end of each interaction.*
- *How old he had felt at the beginning, middle and end of each interaction.*
- *How he had behaved at the beginning, middle and end of each interaction.*
- *How, in retrospect, he might have done things differently.*
- *How the competent, Adult part of him [see page 36] could step up to assist now in a way that it hadn't been able to in the moment of the interaction.*

After a few weeks of diligently journaling about his dealings with his boss, Amir began to realise that if she had been critical of him one day, he would not put any effort into getting things right the next, because, as he put it, what was the point of trying if it wasn't going to be good enough? This would result in a downward spiral of his putting in minimal effort and expecting to be berated, his being berated, and then his putting in even less effort.

Over the weekends when he had two days away from the office, he was able to get out of this unhelpful approach and see things more objectively and rationally. He would return to work on Monday morning filled with enthusiasm to do everything perfectly, but as soon as he received any feedback (even if it was constructive, he was now able to recognise), he would return to his state of despair and despondency.

Poor Amir! That small boy inside him had spent his whole life trying to protect him from the wrath of his father and the scathing attack on his sense of worth by disengaging and not trying his best. He soon started to see that this was a pattern that had played out in all of his jobs, and not just with bosses but with colleagues too. Any advice or comment that was offered to him was heard as an attack by his scared inner child, rather than being received as the constructive input it was meant as. Because of what he had seen and experienced as a child, Amir had been in a long-held observation-expectation-experience dynamic [see page 44] with his boss.

He also realised that he felt and acted like a frightened and often recalcitrant child when he was interacting with his boss. By moving into his Adult state, he was able to listen and hear without becoming defensive, and to explain his thinking and process calmly and confidently enough that she was able to hear him.

With a lot of hard work and mindfulness, Amir was able to stop himself from giving up at the first bit of feedback, and to take it on board and make the suggested changes.

I cannot describe how often I see this in my coaching practice: clients who are at their wits' end about a situation they find seemingly inexplicable and insoluble. They are their usual professional and collected selves until they need to interact with a certain colleague (it doesn't have to be a boss) and then, with no warning, all their emotional buttons are pressed, and they begin to feel and often behave like a frustrated, anxious, scared or angry child. It is unbearably upsetting to feel as powerless as an adult as we felt when we were small.

The truth is that many of us go through what Amir was experiencing. We all have wounds that we're unconsciously trying to heal by unknowingly seeking out or creating situations that replicate the challenging experiences we had in childhood. This could be with a critical, punitive authority figure, or spoiled lazy peers, or team members who always need to be rescued, just like certain relatives.

We go to work, a place where we feel that we should be able to be our best adult selves, and, without being aware of it, we find ourselves playing out all sorts of drama and palaver that reminds us of our childhood. There's the colleague who behaves just like our younger sibling, who leaves everything to the last minute and needs to be bailed out to avert disaster. Or the member of our team who seems to constantly be in a state of emotional turmoil, in need of frequent days off and counselling and a lot of leeway. Or the manager or boss who is critical or demanding or irritable or incapable…

It seems that we're programmed to find (or create) situations that provide us with the opportunity to make sense of what happened to us years ago. But if we don't actively and mindfully do the work of making sense of it, we're destined to keep seeking out the same situation, with the same personalities, and playing out the same scenarios of hurt, disappointment, frustration or worse.

And, just as much as we have unconscious fears and sores that cause us to react to situations from our Child state (see page 36), so does everyone else in the office. It isn't only us trying to heal our childhood injuries, it's all our colleagues as well. Is it any wonder that the workplace can get so fraught at times?

Astoundingly, it takes just one of us responding differently to change the dynamic. Like throwing a pebble into a pond, each mindful and Adult interaction spreads ripples of maturity throughout the organisation.

Think about the last few jobs you have had. Can you identify any patterns or trends in your experience of the workplace?

o   Do you always have horrible bosses, or often take on other people's work, or always feel like an outsider?

o   Can you draw any links between how you feel at work (sometimes or all the time) and how you felt in your childhood?

o   What role are you — unconsciously and almost certainly unwillingly — playing in how any drama may play out at work?

o   How can you break and reset any patterns you have identified?

THE OBSERVATION-EXPECTATION-EXPERIENCE DYNAMIC

I firmly believe that there's a link between what we expect and what we experience. But I think it's more complex than just 'getting what we expect' because what we expect is based on experience or observations. Observations and experiences influence expectations, which then influence experiences…

Obviously, this isn't always the case, but I have observed that it's the case often enough for me to make a simple general rule:

Positive observations + positive experiences = positive expectations
Negative observations + negative experiences = negative expectations

When we have a negative initial experience or observation of a place or a person, it is often enough to cloud all our expectations and thus experiences of that person or place going forward. How many people do you know (including yourself) who will refuse to go back to a restaurant where they had a waiter who was inefficient and offhand in their attentions? Or complain bitterly about having to renew a licence or passport because they expect (and therefore experience) bad service?

Lebo came for coaching to help her get over her fear of her boss and feel more able to have professional and collegial interactions with him. 'I don't know why, but every time I see him or speak to him, I feel anxious and stressed, and I become unable to express myself clearly and calmly. It makes no sense because the rest of the time, and with every other member of staff, even those who are above me in the hierarchy, I am composed and articulate – and quite impressive, if I say so myself.'

The more she described the interaction with her boss, the clearer it became that Lebo went into every interaction she had with him in her frightened Child ego state. Unsurprisingly, he met her from his critical Parent state, which made her more anxious, and him more impatient. It sounded (and looked – her discomfort was evident as she described the interactions) pretty awful.

Because she struggled with only this particular person at work, it seemed there was something deeper going on. I asked her to remember the first exposure she had to her boss. She told me that it had begun when she was making her way into her first day at her new job. As she entered the building, she passed a man in a suit who was walking in circles and shouting into his cellphone. Lebo couldn't hear everything that he was saying (the only thing she heard very clearly was, 'Why do you have to be so irritating and incompetent?') but she could tell that he was very cross. He was radiating impatience and irritability. She gave him a wide berth and continued up to her office, thinking to herself that he seemed to be a very scary and intimidating person. 'I'm pleased I don't have to have anything to do with him,' she remembered saying to herself as she scuttled off.

A couple of hours later, Lebo was invited to attend her first staff tea, only to find, to her horror, that the man in charge of the whole department she had been assigned to was the very same shouty man she encountered that morning. Her heart dropped into her stomach, which was making its way down to her brand-

new shiny work shoes. This did not bode well for her hopes and dreams of a convivial work environment.

All the other team members seemed to get on well with him and chatted easily to him over coffee and cake, but Lebo stayed as far away from him as possible. When the time came for her to be introduced to him (Lucas was his name), she shuffled over feeling like a frightened child in imminent danger of being given the kind of scolding she had witnessed him giving a few hours earlier. Lebo was so anxious, she became utterly tongue-tied and unable to make eye contact. She was, in her own words, 'a gibbering wreck who came across as inarticulate, incapable and unprofessional'. And it had stayed that way since.

As we unpacked this incident, Lebo came to understand that her first impression of Lucas had been so powerful that it had created an enduring expectation of him as being tetchy, critical and more than a little intolerant. Despite all other evidence – seeing him being kind and supportive to a staff member in distress, hearing her colleagues talk about what great guy and brilliant boss he was – Lebo's expectation, and thus her experience, of him was very different.

It didn't matter that the only time Lebo had ever seen Lucas raise his voice was that time in the foyer, whenever she had to have any direct dealings with him, she expected him to be that angry, scary man she'd seen on her first day and he almost always became that man after a few minutes of interacting with her.

The way to break a damaging observation-expectation-experience dynamic is to identify, understand and dismantle the unhelpful patterns. We started with identifying what Lebo had observed, then I invited her to think about the assumptions she had made on the strength of that first observation of Lucas, and finally I asked her to consider her unconscious expectations and behaviour that resulted from the observation and assumptions.

Lebo's reflections were very enlightening. What she had observed was an irate man shouting into his cellphone. What she had assumed was that Lucas was impatient, critical and somewhat scary. As a result, her unconscious expectation was that she was going to get shouted at and criticised for being irritating and incompetent, and her fear and anxiety about getting into trouble did indeed *make her behave in an irritating and incompetent manner.*

Armed with the information about the observation-expectation-experience dynamic, Lebo proceeded with finding evidence that disproved her assumptions and expectations about Lucas. She came up with a long list of times that she had subsequently observed him being patient and kind and understanding and helpful – the opposite of angry and shouty – even when some of her colleagues were being irritating and incompetent.

With this new information and evidence about Lucas, Lebo was able to see that her initial observation was an anomaly, and that Lucas wasn't that terrifying and terrible man she expected (and experienced) him to be. She could appreciate that he was very different from her first impression of him, and could calm the anxious Child inside her enough to understand and take responsibility for her own role in the fractious conversations they had been having.

Lebo practised preparing herself to interact with Lucas as her Adult self; she imagined several scenarios in her mind and played them out in front of the mirror. The next time she met with him, she was able to start the conversation in a calm, rational and competent way, and he was able to reciprocate calmly and rationally and appreciatively.

In time, she built up the courage to ask Lucas what had angered him so on that fateful day, and he told her he was shouting at the (irritating and incompetent) panelbeater who had been taking days longer than necessary to fix a small dent in his car. What an eye-opener that was for Lebo, who learned an important lesson about making assumptions based on observing only half of the story.

This is the power of expectation and how it affects experience. Because, as American 'father of positive thinking' Norman Vincent Peale observed, 'We tend to get what we expect.' This is true not just because we're inclined to look for evidence that supports our expectation ('all men are unreliable' makes us hyper-alert to any man arriving a few minutes late; 'the youth are lazy' means we only see them staring at their phones and look past their output and contribution), but also because we – almost always unconsciously – behave in a way that makes it almost impossible for that expectation not to be met.

With Lebo, this meant switching into an anxious, awkward, frightened Child who was so scared of being shouted at by Lucas that she mumbled and avoided eye contact whenever she spoke to him. And, as we know from transactional analysis, this brought out the impatient, irascible critical Parent in Lucas.

Think about an observation-expectation-experience dynamic you've had at work and/or with your colleagues (or in your home life). Remember the incident that was the foundation for the consequent expectations and experiences. Ask yourself:

o   What did you observe?
o   What assumptions did you make?
o   What did the observation and assumptions lead you to expect?
o   What have you experienced as a result of these expectations?

It's helpful, also, to ask yourself what ego state may have been triggered during the observation and assumptions, and how that ego state may have persisted in the expectations and experiences you've had as a consequence.

Now, look for evidence that is contrary to, and therefore disproves, your own expectations and experiences. Find as many clues as possible.

Finally, update your expectations and practise how you can change your experiences by coming at it from your best, Adult, self.

As you examine your unconscious expectations of and for relationships and experiences at work (and everywhere), you should start to understand how you may have unknowingly and unwittingly played a hand in allowing or encouraging your expectations and fears to come about.

This is not an invitation to blame yourself or beat yourself up if you start to notice that your expectations may have contributed to your experience! Rather, it's an opportunity to recognise unhelpful assumptions and expectations so that you can replace them with more helpful (and truer) ones.

Impostor syndrome

'I keep expecting them to realise they've made a mistake and say they're reversing my promotion/salary increase/transfer...' I hear this kind of statement far too often from my clients, across the board.

When I probe a little by asking why they think this might happen, there's never a good reason, and even less often is there a chance that their fears will be realised. The people who have this fear are almost always well qualified, very experienced, extremely competent and highly valued. Their fears are not based on fact, but are more to do with impostor syndrome.

In 1978 clinical psychologists Pauline Rose Clance and Suzanne Imes identified what they termed the 'impostor phenomenon'. They described what is now referred to as 'impostor syndrome' as an experience of anxiety about and doubting of our competence and abilities – being convinced that we're about to be outed for being a fraud.

People with impostor syndrome find it hard to believe that their accomplishments and successes are due to anything other than luck and possibly a little bit of sleight of hand – they've managed to keep the illusion of competence going for long enough to fool some people some of the time, but this will surely end soon. They don't allow their strengths and super-powers (see page 115) to take centre stage because they're worried that they don't deserve the attention that will result. No matter how much they achieve, they don't feel confident or competent, and nor do they feel the joy of success and achievement, as they're always expecting to be exposed as inadequate.

Even though impostor syndrome is something that's ascribed mostly to women, recent research has shown that men and women are equally likely to experience it. I believe it's something that all 'adult children' (see page 26) are especially prone to, for a number of reasons related to the characteristics that are common to so many of us: we judge ourselves without mercy, and we constantly seek approval and affirmation but often don't trust it when it comes; we're our harshest critics, and we never quite believe that we're adequate; and, because we often saw confusing and unpredictable behaviour when we were growing up, we guess what normal is, which makes it hard for us to assess whether or not our feelings, worries and anxieties are to be expected or if they're specific to us. We don't realise that most people have some level and degree of performance anxiety – we think it's just us.

Because so many adult children have a foundational belief that we aren't good enough ('If I were better, it would be better'), it's hard to trust that anything we do or achieve is worthy and enduring. We struggle to ask for help and advice, so we often have little sense of how our work is perceived, and we keep expecting any feedback we get to be negative rather than positive.

Adult children are great pretenders (we pretend to be happy or able or willing when we may not be), so we're in a constant state of anxiety that we're going to be found out, and reveal what we fear to be the truth – that we aren't what people believe us to be.

Even when we are recognised for a job well done or are given a promotion or asked to lead an important project, that small insecure child inside us can't allow us to believe that we're seen as anything other than deficient and possibly even pitiful. We tell ourselves that the praise is because they feel sorry for us, or we got the promotion because there were no other candidates. We live in constant fear of being discovered or outed as incompetent or inadequate.

While there's no doubt that the anxiety that fuels many people is at the root of much impostor syndrome, it's equally true that the working environment and organisational culture and climate (see page 136) play enormous roles too, resulting in impostor syndrome not only for women, but for anyone who doesn't fit the 'traditional' image of the office worker: a white, heterosexual male. Anyone on the receiving end of discrimination and microaggressions – racism, sexism, homophobia, etc – is vulnerable to a feeling of not being good enough, a buying into of the 'if I were better, it would be better' story, and therefore to experiencing impostor syndrome for at least some period in their careers.

It seems too great a coincidence that so many of my coaching clients who come to me for burnout-recovery coaching are also sufferers of impostor syndrome. Sure, some of the overlap is down to personality and driven by the internal environment of the individuals, but we can't ignore the organisational environments that exacerbate anxiety and self-judgement.

Feeling uncomfortable, unsure and even a bit anxious about the quality and impact of the work we do is pretty much true of all people at some stage of their career – and especially in the early years when we're just starting out, or when we've been promoted into a new and unfamiliar role. It's an indication of how badly we want to do well: if we didn't care about our jobs or our performance, we wouldn't experience any apprehension about not being good enough. But when that anxiety turns from fear of the unfamiliar to a loss of faith in our abilities, it becomes a major challenge.

Perhaps the worst aspect of the condition is the way it can prevent people from growing and finding meaning in new and rewarding projects that are offered to them at work. When the fear of failure is all-encompassing, it spoils the enjoyment and sense of achievement we should bask in when we're recognised and given new opportunities.

ADDRESSING IMPOSTOR SYNDROME

How do we show impostor syndrome the door, and allow ourselves to believe in and celebrate our achievements?

Speak up

The first step, as with all challenges of this nature, is admitting that you have a problem. There's nothing quite as liberating and worry-reducing as speaking your fears and anxieties out loud. It's a bit like opening the door and showing the frightened child that there isn't a monster hiding in the cupboard: when we shine a light on our fears – or say them aloud – we minimise them with the truth.

'I'm worried that my boss is going to think I'm incompetent', said out loud in the light of day, sounds far more ridiculous to the recently promoted manager with a record of almost faultless performance reviews than it does when she whispers it to herself in the dead of night.

The other benefit to speaking up is that you will almost certainly come to the comforting realisation that you're not the only one who questions your abilities and worries that you will be 'found out' – some of the people you speak to will astonish you by admitting that they've felt (or feel) the same way.

Ask for help

Now that you've told yourself the truth, you can ask for help to manage your anxiety. This help can come in the form of regular meetings with a group of peers, mentorship from a more experienced colleague, talking to a trusted friend or finding a coach.

Look back at what you've achieved

This is one of the first things the person helping you will probably ask you to do. Make a list of all the things you've ever managed to achieve and get right in your life and in your career – things that now, in hindsight, you're able to trust you did a good job with. If you're struggling to remember any, ask a trusted friend or colleague to help you remember your achievements.

Reframe the anxiety

Everybody – especially everybody who is invested in their work and wants to do it well – feels anxiety and fear about not being good enough at least some of the time. It's an indication of how invested you are in your work and how much you value the opportunities you're given. If you never felt any sense of trepidation about not doing a good enough job, it would show that your performance was of little consequence to you.

If you can shift your understanding of the anxiety from a fear of being outed as an imposter to a deep desire to do well ('investment in success syndrome'), perhaps you will feel less paralysed by it.

Be kind to yourself

Accept that you're only human and there may be some things that you don't do perfectly at first or all the time, and allow yourself the space and time to make mistakes, and to learn and grow from them. Change your internal dialogue from one of critical judgement to one of kind inquisitiveness: 'I should have done better' to 'What could I have done differently?'

A lifetime of experiences and conditioning has made most of us adopt at least some of the characteristics and behaviours covered in this chapter. Through our early years we learned to look after others, attempted to please the people we love, tried to be self-sufficient, did whatever we felt we needed to do to stay safe. And many of us have unknowingly taken these behaviours into the grownup world of work, where they have varying degrees of success or hindrance. With growing self-awareness and commitment to be mindfully Adult, we can change our experience of work to be not just healthy, but also healing.

Can you think of two or three 'tiny' habits that will help you to improve your level of satisfaction in this area and allow your Wheel of Work to give you a smoother ride?

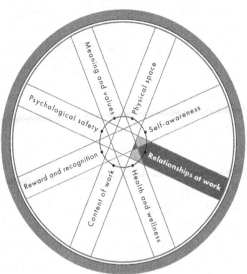

Relationships and community at work

No man is an island. A trouble shared is a trouble halved. A person is a person because of other people. It doesn't matter what the saying is, or who says it, the sentiment is the same: people need people. We all need some degree of community. We need to see and be seen, hear and be heard, notice and appreciate and be noticed and appreciated – but without feeling overwhelmed, over-scrutinised and constantly judged.

Most of us spend more than half of our waking life at work or working, and one of the ways we can ensure that all that time feels meaningful as well as productive is by having satisfying interactions with the people around us.

Some of us are 'solopreneurs' who work alone and go for hours or days without seeing another person. Some of us are part of large teams or organisations, surrounded by people every minute of the day. And the rest of us fit somewhere in between. No matter who we are or where and how we work, we are inclined to underestimate the impact that isolation or inclusion can have on our happiness, creativity and productivity.

If you are not seeing enough people, or are seeing too much of people who are not right for you, you may find yourself feeling lonely, isolated and disconnected. When we feel alienated from others, work (and life) can begin to feel more overwhelming, more frightening, less meaningful. But when we feel connected and appreciated, magical, synergistic things can happen.

'Synergy' refers to an interaction between two or more entities that results in something that is greater than the sum of the individual parts. Synergy happens when the kinds of ideas and creative energy that result from a group of people thinking, talking and working together, are far more ingenious and inspired than would have been possible for one person thinking alone. It's what happens, for example, when you have a mental block about something, and as soon as you talk to a colleague about it, the answer miraculously presents itself to you. Or when you have a brainstorming meeting and come up with so many weird and wonderful ideas that you leave the room feeling excited, energised and engaged with your fellow brainstormers.

A sad fallout of the pandemic lockdowns was that the opportunities for synergy were greatly compromised while most of us were working remotely and individually. The opportunities to shoot the breeze and chat creatively about problems and solutions didn't present themselves. We learned to rely on ourselves and our own thinking, and many of us got out of the habit of asking for cerebral help and ideas.

I believe that we need to consciously and concertedly recreate the synergistic spaces that we so urgently need to help us heal from the trauma of isolation and separation, and to reignite our creative sparks.

Crafting your community

There is no doubt that spending time with people who inspire and motivate you – and contribute to a sense of belonging – can help you to be more productive, more fulfilled and generally happier. Feeling connected to others can help to generate synergy and enthusiasm for and about your work in a manner that can't be created by any other means. We need to create communities that contribute to wellbeing at work, not only to reduce and prevent burnout and alienation, but also to promote more creative and effective work.

Kyle found absolutely no comfort or pleasure in his job. His work was stressful and seemingly relentless, and he came for coaching because he was worried that he might blow up like a pressure cooker that isn't able to let off steam in a controlled way.

We identified that what made everything seem so much worse was the fact that he was lonely at work.

An only child, Kyle was so used to being self-sufficient in his games and his studies that in adulthood he exuded an air of 'I don't need anyone' without even being aware of it. Consequently, he not only didn't have many – or any – work friends, he also didn't have any thinking partners or people whom he could ask for advice or feedback.

Because it was such a familiar situation for him to be in, he hadn't even realised how lonely and isolated he had been feeling at work.

Kyle committed to building relationships at work. He started small – creating opportunities to connect by arriving at meetings a bit early and staying back afterwards for a couple of minutes to chat, rather than rushing back to his office the minute the meetings closed. He very bravely started to share his thoughts in those meetings. After a while, and even more bravely, he took his lunch into the staff dining area a couple of times a week instead of eating at his desk every day.

Through slowly and gently making himself more visible and less aloof – by joining in the chat about the weekend's sports and the like – he was able to build some connections. Within a couple of months, not only did he have people to chat to over lunch and tea breaks, he also had a couple of people he trusted to give him time and thinking space when he needed to bounce an idea off someone else.

Work became much more enjoyable for Kyle. Not only did he feel less lonely, he also became less stressed, as he'd built relationships with a couple of trusted colleagues with whom he could let off steam. As a result of all this, his work

became more interesting, and more creative and rewarding. He began to reap the
rewards of the connection and synergies he was building.

On the opposite end of the spectrum to Kyle, some of my clients struggle to get their work done because they're spending *too much* time on relationship and community. For very gregarious people, people who need to be where the action is, or people who are happy for any excuse to avoid doing their work, community at work can become too much of a good thing.

There's always a challenge in finding the balance that's right for you and ensuring that you create and maintain that balance.

One of the hardest things for me when I started working for and by myself 20 years ago was the absence of a community. In true 'adult child' fashion, I had gone from one extreme to the other, and replaced too much workplace socialising with none at all. Even though I was pleased to have left what was becoming an increasingly stale job and work environment, I missed my colleagues.

Despite being an introvert, I'm a chatty sort and place high value on talking to people and feeling a sense of belonging and kinship. After a couple of months of working from home as an independent consultant, my productivity tanked and my anxiety levels rose. I had no one to pass the time of day with, to complain to about whatever was getting on my nerves, or with whom to talk through a tricky concept. I found myself catching up on the news, having numerous restorative naps and even doing the laundry when I should have been concentrating on my work deliverables.

As soon as I persuaded a couple of friends who were in the same position to share a rented office with me – happily, these days it's relatively easy to find communal working spaces that are available to rent by the hour, day, week or month – my productivity returned and my anxiety dropped. I went from dreading my work to looking forward to doing it in the company of others. Since then, I've always found ways to – at least some of the time – ensure some or other form of community while or where I work. I see my in-person coaching clients from a set of rooms occupied by other coaches and counsellors who all enjoy a quick chat between clients. On what we call 'working Wednesdays', I meet my friend Jenny in a coffee shop, and we spend the mornings working on our projects – separately but together – in between coffee and conversation.

It's important to remember that everyone is different, and we all have different needs and desires. Some of us work well alone and others need to be around people – not just any people but people who we feel happy and safe with, connected to, inspired by. Some of us can ignore the negative effects or overstimulation that comes from being around people who irritate or overwhelm us; others are deeply affected by others' energies and attitudes.

How happy are you with the kind and extent of community you have in your work life? Ask yourself:

o   Do you feel lonely and isolated (maybe you work for yourself, by yourself, or maybe you have nothing in common with any of your colleagues)?

o   Do you feel overstimulated or negatively stimulated by your colleagues?

o   If you're not as satisfied as you would like to be, what can you do to improve your levels of satisfaction with your community at work?

o   Is there a way you can speak to a manager or supervisor about being put onto a team with people who will bring out the best in you and your work?

o   If you work by and for yourself, can you join a professional group, start a co-op with similar professionals, go and work in your local coffee shop...?

o   If none of these (or any other ideas that you may have) work, can you arrange for a friend/s to come and have lunch with you a few days a week? Communities outside of work can also contribute to your happiness and fulfilment at work.

Relationships at work are wonderful when they are fun, kind and supportive. They can be a place of refuge and sustenance, particularly when work is hard, and projects are stressful. Many of the big organisations know this, which is why they put so much attention on and resources into team-building and other strategies to help workers feel that they are having fun at work, rather than missing out on a good time when they are staying late at the office. For many professionals, their early years in the workplace are where they forge some of their strongest and most enduring friendships.

Unfortunately, not all office communities are cool and cooperative; some are competitive, combative and even adversarial. Those managers who don't pay active attention to the people dynamics can find themselves in a situation where there is less synergy and more antagonism among their staff; again, not so much of the psychological safety.

Even in the best-imagined organisations, there are some people in charge, and others who are not; some people who get to make decisions and others who have to implement those decisions; some staff members who get to talk, and others who have to listen.

Cliques

Remember when you were an adolescent and no one really knew who decided who was in and who was out? The same is unfortunately often true at work.

It's an unwritten law that some people are more important and worthier than others. If we're lucky, we have our own set of friends and supporters to hang out with, to joke with, to feel a part of something bigger with. And if we're unlucky, work can feel like a lonely and alienating space: for some people, the role of the outsider is thrust upon them.

This is the power of cliques.

A work clique is a collection of colleagues who spend most of their work time with each other and often get together to socialise outside of working hours too. We all tend to seek out people who look and seem similar to ourselves, and organisations will typically have cliques made up of individuals who have common interests, common backgrounds, common experiences in the company, common ideas, etc. These highly bonded groups of friends, while creating a wonderful sense of belonging and kinship for the individuals within, can seem very exclusionary and exclusive for the people who are on the outside.

While cliques generally begin from a desire to be with people who understand and sympathise with each other, they can turn nasty – not for the people in the clique, but for those who feel excluded from it. Just as feeling uncool and undeserving was so stressful and isolating when we were teenagers, so being in no or the 'wrong' clique at work can have a very negative impact on our experience of work.

At worst, the wrong kinds of cliques can contribute to othering, and to sidelining competent and creative individuals just because they don't fit the profile of the 'in group'; at best, they can result in narrow thinking due to a lack of diversity and experience.

'Sometimes I feel like I'm back in high school. There are the cool kids, the clever kids, the in crowd, and the rest of us.' Lindi was expressing what so many of us have felt at various times in our careers – that feeling that there are only a chosen few who get all the attention and recognition; that sense of being peripheral and coming a poor second to the A-team.

Lindi had been in her job for a few months before she became aware of this 'us and them' nature of many of the dynamics in her organisation. At first she thought she was imagining the giggling, the gossiping and the sudden silences when she walked into a room occupied by what she came to call 'the chosen ones'. But as time went on, she acknowledged that it really was happening. There was a group of people who, because they had the ear and attention of the boss, felt that they were better than everyone else.

For Lindi, who had fought many odds to land what she thought was her dream job, the experience of feeling judged and sidelined was devastating. Her instinct, when she identified what was happening, was to resign and find another job. 'I don't compete, I retreat,' she explained to me.

Although it doesn't always feel like it, the workplace is not high school. As adults, we have the agency to make choices about who we hang out with and how we conduct ourselves. We can choose how we want to present ourselves to the world and to our colleagues.

Lindi and I worked on banishing the part of her that felt like an anxious adolescent who wanted to play truant to stay away from the hurt, and summoned up her Adult self [see page 36] to help her figure out how best to manage the situation. She decided that she was going to give herself six months to see if she could build her own supportive community at the office, and if she wasn't able to do so, then she would start looking for another job. This decision allowed her to feel that she did have a choice about where she was, while also empowering her to try and make a difference to her experience without reacting impulsively and emotionally, and running away.

Lindi started off her campaign by identifying a couple of colleagues who she thought she may like to make friends with. Even though it was scary and hard for a person as shy and introverted as Lindi, she forced herself to connect with these colleagues by offering to make them a cup of tea when she made her own, asking them about themselves, and voicing her appreciation of them when it was appropriate, whether it was about the points they made in a meeting or the shoes they were wearing.

Gradually, she started building authentic relationships with two of her peers, and within a few months she didn't care what the chosen ones were doing, because she had her own crew to hang out and giggle and share stories with – although she vowed never to let herself and her work friends ever do anything to make anyone else feel excluded and alienated the way she used to. And I believe that she will carry this through.

Anyone who has been on the outside looking in knows how alienating and awful cliques can be. Having a set of work friends is wonderful – we all love to have people we can share things with during the working day – but there's a big difference between a respectful, supportive and fun friendship group, and a clique that is like a members-only club. Lindi was very aware of this, which is why she chose to have a friendship group that could expand to include others when appropriate, rather than a clique.

So, what can you do to minimise the impact of cliques in your workplace? What can you do to make sure that you mindfully build on the positives and minimise the negatives of cliques and groups in your office?

It's important to understand that the workplace is always going to be a playground for some people, and no matter how nice you are and how hard you try to be their friend and colleague, you're not going to get very far. It's a waste of your precious time and energy trying to change that. Be polite but save your energy for doing the kind of work that satisfies you, and connecting with people who appreciate you and who make you feel you've spent your day well. And stay out of the drama!

Drama in the workplace

Buhle was the oldest child in a single-parent household. She had three younger siblings and a permanently stressed and exhausted father who, like most parents, was doing the best he could with the limited emotional and material resources that he had available. Clearly overwhelmed, he relied on Buhle to shoulder a large part of the burden of child-minding and raising her siblings. She got into the habit of helping the younger children with their homework, making supper, and ensuring that everyone was fed and bathed before she began to attend to her own homework after dinner every night.

Despite, or perhaps because of, her many demands, Buhle was able to finish school with good results and study for a degree that got her into a job that she loved and was very good at.

She came for coaching because she was having to work longer and longer hours to try and get on top of her workload. She never used to mind staying late at the office to work; it was nice and quiet, and she was often at her most productive when everyone had left to go home for the day. She would spend a large part of every working day listening to, advising and bailing out her friends and team-mates at work, and it was only after her colleagues had left the office that she was able to settle down to a couple of hours of productivity.

But Buhle had recently embarked on a promising new relationship with a lovely, supportive person – someone, she realised, with whom she wanted to spend longer evenings instead of the couple of hours that remained after she'd completed her own and everyone else's work. She wanted to work on getting more done in the hours she was paid to do her work in. And to do that, she had to stop dropping her own agenda in order to serve others'.

Through coaching, Buhle was able to recognise that she had been replicating in the workplace the drama triangle that had evolved during her childhood. She was a rescuer by nature, which is why she found herself stepping in and doing the work of so many of her colleagues. A separate but related problem was that her boundaries were leaky. She was allowing everyone and everything into her space – and on their terms.

Stephen Karpman was a transactional analyst who came up with 'the drama triangle' to describe and explain the dynamic that so many of us get into in many of our relationships and interactions.

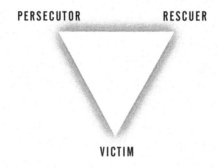

This upside-down triangle shows how we can get into a situation with another person where each of us feels either like a victim who is being bullied and/or wanting to be rescued, or a persecutor who is bullying the victim, or like we are being expected to rescue the other person. Two of the roles are being played out at any time and, because the drama triangle is very volatile, we can switch between the roles in a split second.

In a classic drama triangle, there is a co-dependent relationship between what is often an addict (the victim) and the person or people they expect to be rescued by (their partner, parents or other people close to them).

If the rescuing stops, the victim generally turns into a persecutor and bullies the other party back into rescuing them. They can do this either by outright, aggressive bullying, or by becoming bullies dressed up as victims (what I call 'bully-victims') who passive-aggressively bully by saying things like, 'If you don't help me then I will be fired, and my children will starve, and we'll lose our house, and it will all be your fault.' Bully-victims make life very difficult for us because we don't know whether to run away from them as quickly as possible or whether we need to rescue them.

Occasionally, the rescuer becomes the bully and turns on the victim in a surprisingly punitive way, which most often makes the victim even less capable of taking charge of their own life... and so the drama continues.

Looked at from the point of view of our 'ego states' (see page 36), when we're in the rescuer position, we are in our nurturing Parent ego state. When we get tired of being the rescuer and we turn into the persecutor, we're moving from our nurturing Parent to our critical Parent ego state. And when we're in the victim role, we're in our Child ego state – either frightened Child ('I'm sorry, please don't hurt me') or rebellious Child ('You're not the boss of me; I'll show you').

There are no Adults in the drama triangle. Therefore, the way to get out and stay out of the drama is to be in our Adult ego state. If we step into our Adult state and step away from the drama triangle, we leave behind the possibility of drama, because if there is only one person in the triangle, there can be no drama.

When we get into our Adult state, we are (in the words of psychiatrist Thomas Harris's 1967 book *I'm OK – You're OK*) okay: we are able to be mindful of the fact that we can look after ourselves; we can make our own choices and take our own actions without needing to be rescued or looked after by anyone else. We are also able to see that everyone else is also an okay Adult, equally capable of making their own way in the world.

As Adults, we can recognise when we may need help, and are able to ask for it capably, rather than expecting or demanding to be rescued. And we can choose if and how we would like to help people in need, rather than feeling compelled to be the rescuer.

It's important to understand and be aware of the fact that there's an enormous difference between helping and rescuing. Helping is empowering for both the helper and the person being helped, but rescuing is disempowering for both the person being rescued and the rescuer who is set up for ongoing demands. Rescuing endlessly perpetuates the drama triangle.

When we rescue everybody else, we make a victim of ourselves, because the more we rescue, the more we need to rescue, as Buhle realised.

Often, we don't reach our own goals because we're too busy 'helping' other people to reach theirs. We get into the habit of looking after everybody else, and because of this others-centredness, we forget to look after and remember our own needs – we put everybody else's demands, whether they're real or imagined, above our own.

As Buhle identified, when we forget to remember ourselves, it means that we don't have enough time or energy or memory to meet our own needs, or to do our own work. And then we get resentful.

The drama triangle plays out in our daily lives and interactions in many and varied ways. When, like Buhle, we rescue a team member by doing their work for them, because we can't resist or don't have the patience to listen to their hard-luck, the-dog-ate-my-homework stories, we are in the drama triangle. When we lend the colleague who never comes out on their salary more and more money, until one day, faced with our own financial worries, we lose it with them and shout – and then feel terrible and hand over yet more money – we are in the drama triangle. When we're humiliated by a manager who takes out their own insecurity or unhappiness by belittling us in a staff meeting, we are in the drama triangle.

It's important to understand that no one gets into this dynamic on purpose; the interactions that play out are almost always entirely unconscious, which only makes the manipulations that take place more powerful.

The drama triangle is both unhealthy and unsustainable. The rescuer gets tired of having to do the rescuing, and becomes angry and resentful. The victim gets sick of feeling unworthy, and becomes angry and resentful. The persecutor becomes so exhausted from all the bullying, they get sick and even angrier.

Most of us are in multiple drama triangles with many people in every area of our lives – at home, with friends, in our communities and, of course, at work.

Being in the drama triangle at work is a one-way street to burnout and a breakdown of relationships, but until we become aware of what is going on and how it is playing out, it is almost impossible to stop the drama. As soon as we're able to understand and leave the drama triangles, we're able to make work work better for us.

In order for Buhle to ensure she went home at the same time as everybody else, leaving a clean desk behind her, she had to set some boundaries around her time and availability, and stop rushing in with solutions whenever her colleagues asked her to solve their problems. She needed to introduce and maintain some strong barriers around her time and attention, while also ensuring that she enabled her colleagues to come up with their own answers and solutions.

First, she created some clear but kind workable boundaries by making herself available for questions, discussions and requests for assistance during her 'consultation hours', which she set to be from 3pm to 5pm every afternoon. This was the time of day that she knew she was at her least productive and, without constant interruptions throughout the rest of the day, would have cleared her desk of her own work and be able to pay attention to whoever needed her.

Second, Buhle trained herself to respond to pleas from colleagues to solve their problems for them by asking 'How can I help you?' rather than rushing in with the solution for them.

These two approaches worked beautifully together to save Buhle's time, energy and goodwill, while also empowering her colleagues. By making herself unavailable except for during those two hours in the afternoons, Buhle ensured that her peers drew on their own creativity and resources to come up with their own solutions to problems they would otherwise have expected her to solve.

When they came to her with whatever problems they hadn't already solved while waiting for her to become available, she resisted the urge to reach a speedy resolution by offering a solution and instead asked 'How can I help?' which encouraged the wannabe victims to step into their Adult ego state and think calmly and competently about the situation before identifying a solution. A few of the solutions her colleagues came up with required some assistance from Buhle, but often she was only required to give feedback on approaches or progress.

'How can I help you?' is a powerful question. It ensures that the person who is being asked it feels heard and taken seriously, but it also, crucially, expresses confidence that they know not only what problems they are faced with, but also how to solve them. Asking the question also creates the space to choose if and how you are able and willing to give the assistance asked for. It's empowering and enlightening for both parties.

When we're busy and stressed, and when we're predisposed to saving people from themselves, it often feels like it will be quicker and more effective to give someone the answer rather than asking the important questions, and so we're inclined to rush in with all the solutions. But when we do that, we're creating a self-perpetuating cycle of needing to rescue people, because we don't take the time and make the effort to help them to save themselves. A little bit of patience and upfront expense of time and energy is well worth it for the results that unfold as people become more competent and less needy.

THE CREATOR TRIANGLE

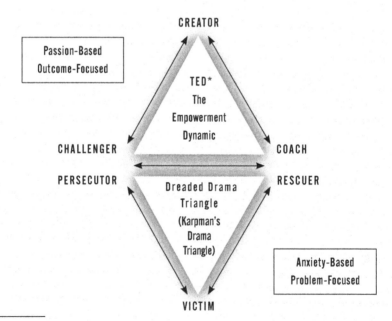

Image courtesy of David Emerald and the Power of TED*
www.powerofted.com

In response to what they call the 'dreaded drama triangle', life coaches David Emerald and Donna Zajonc flipped it around and came up with the creator triangle. While the drama triangle is (according to them) anxiety-based and problem-focused, their creator triangle is passion-based and outcome-focused.

In this new, more empowering and sustainable model, what was the victim is now at the top of the triangle – the hero of the story – and has moved into a creator role. The erstwhile rescuer and persecutor (now the challenger and the coach) are both below the creator, forming a solid foundation for creativity. In this model of interaction, everyone is feeling (and acting) like able, adequate and creative Adults.

The rescuer-turned-coach asks, 'How can I help?' or 'What help do you need?' rather than rushing in to fix things. The persecutor-turned-challenger asks, 'Are you sure you need me to do this?' or 'Let's look at this from a different angle', instead of complaining or berating when faced with neediness or inability. And the victim-turned-creator states, 'This is what I need help with…' or 'Please can you help me with…?' rather than helplessly waiting to be rescued.

What is even more powerful about this dynamic is that if just one person shifts into their new role, they empower the people they have been stuck in dramas with to do the same. When Buhle stopped rescuing and started coaching, for example, she encouraged her colleagues to become the creators of their own solutions. When Amir was able to think creatively about himself and his work, he was able to see his boss as a challenger who was encouraging him to be a more active creator.

Are you in any drama triangles at work? Ask yourself:
- Think about the colleagues or managers you try to avoid the most – what about them and your interaction with them is making you try to keep yourself away?
- Try to identify the dynamic you are getting into with them – are you rescuing, persecuting or being victimised by them?
- What does your calm, rational Adult self know you need to do to step out of and stay out of any drama triangles you may be in?
- Once you have identified the dramas you're involved in and the roles you've been playing, ask yourself what you can do to flip the dynamic around.
- How can you shift from victim to creator, or from persecutor to challenger, or from rescuer to coach?
- How can you tighten up your boundaries so that you can stay out of the drama?

Boundaries at work

When I left my last full-time employment 20 years ago, and once I had set up my shared office system of working that allowed me to be as productive as possible, I couldn't believe how much I managed to get done every day. What used to take me days I was now achieving in hours. It felt nothing short of miraculous.

It made me realise just how much time was wasted on the 'informal processes' that were at play in my previous job – the chat in the kitchen while making coffee, the conversations about work projects before and after the formal meetings, the bonding with colleagues over birthday teas and end-of-week drinks. I'm a big fan of these informal processes – they're all part of the glue that sticks the communities at work together. But when these unofficial interactions take up more time than the paid work, they can become a hindrance rather than a help.

I realised that, before I left that job, this had been happening more and more: people would come into my office to complain about various things (a lot and often), and I was on various committees, which meant frequent meetings, which in turn meant more and more downtime around those meetings. And because I was bored with much of the work I was doing, I not only welcomed these interruptions but actively sought them out.

The problem was one of boundaries. The organisation wasn't great with them (I can't remember a meeting that started or ended on time), and nor was I. I didn't just let the complainers come into my office and waste my time and energy, I invited them in. Instead of arriving at my meetings five minutes before their scheduled starting time and leaving as soon as they were finished, I hung around before and after, drinking tea and 'networking' for far too long and with no professional gain.

I often hear similar stories from clients: they're pulled in so many different directions when they're at the office that they aren't able to concentrate on the deliverables they're expected to produce. Not managing to do all their work while they're at work means that they take work home to complete after hours and over weekends, and this means not getting enough time to rest and recharge. With ever-diminishing energy reserves, they're less focused when they're in the office, more open to time-wasters and less productive... It's a vicious cycle of not enough time spent on work at work, leading to not enough time spent on recharging after work, leading to even less time working at work.

Now that I'm a burnout recovery and prevention coach, I'm very aware of the importance of strong and healthy boundaries to ensure that not only do we get the job done, but we get it done in a way that doesn't exhaust and drain us. While we need connections and community at work, we also need to be mindful about limiting our interruptions and not allowing our interactions to get in the way of our output.

Boundaries are essentially barriers; they are the partitions we put up so that we can protect ourselves and what belongs to us. This applies to not just our physical possessions but also our time, our emotions, our energy – even our thoughts and ideas. If our boundaries are too rigid, they keep out the good as well as the bad. If they're not rigid enough, they let everything in and out like a sieve, leaving us with nothing.

The best boundaries are ones that allow for entry and exit; rather than building a solid wall that no one and nothing can get through, leaving you isolated and alone, it is best to have a figurative door or gate in your wall so that you're able to open it when, how and to whom you want to.

Kyle's boundaries were initially so strong that they were impenetrable. As a result of not allowing anything or anyone in – or out – he had a build-up of negative emotions and stress with no way of letting them out, and nothing good to offset them. It was only when he consciously chose to open the door to some of his colleagues that he was able to let out some of the bad and allow in a lot of good.

My 'open-door' approach in my last job meant that there was a steady flow of people and their problems drifting in and out of my working day, eroding not only my productive time but also my attention and energy. I had fallen into the trap of allowing in too much, leaving me depleted and overwhelmed.

Even though it can feel very hard to say 'no' we must learn to protect ourselves, and our time, energy and goodwill, by building and maintaining healthy boundaries. But there are so many different ways our boundaries can be violated that it is sometimes hard to know when it's happening.

Imagine if you had a neighbour who kept letting themselves into your home and telling you how to wash your dishes? Or who kept bringing you their dirty dishes to wash for them? It's pretty clear that this isn't acceptable behaviour, and you would probably quite easily be able to say 'no' to it.

It's a lot harder to have clear and confident boundaries when things are less obvious: when you receive an urgent email at midnight and feel obliged to respond immediately, for example, or when your work WhatsApp group pings on the weekend, or when your best friend sends you memes and cute cat videos throughout the day. It isn't only people who demand our attention and erode our boundaries; we're often distracted and thrown off course by intrusions from inanimate sources such as emails and social-media alerts.

While information technology has been a great development, it also makes it harder for us to set strong boundaries between work and home. It's just too easy to check our emails, respond to questions or do some extra research for that report on our smartphone and from the comfort of our sitting room.

Clear boundaries around and within work have always been a struggle for most of us, but as a result of the recent change in workspaces, from brick-and-mortar buildings to virtual offices, this has become a whole lot worse. We used to have natural boundaries in the form of commuting time to and from work and set working hours with clear and defined tea and lunch breaks which encouraged us to work at work and be at home at home, but many of these organic intermissions have been seriously eroded. Now, many of us have got into the habit of starting work almost as soon as we wake up, and working long, uninterrupted hours, switching from one online meeting to the next, all without taking breaks for nourishment, connection or recharging.

It's no wonder so many of us are feeling alienated from our work and are finding less and less satisfaction in doing it.

We need to pay urgent attention to resurrecting our boundaries so that we can bring some balance and satisfaction back into our lives, and work and live in a sustainable way.

Look back at your 'not working at work' list you drew up on page 12. Which of those items are boundary-related?

As with most things in life, there will be some boundaries that will be pretty easy to tighten up and others that are more complex. Identify the easier things you can do to tighten up your boundaries by reducing the irritations and interruptions that you allow into your space — but don't forget to allow some good in!

Here are some ideas:
○ Figure out when you're at your most productive and be vigilant about keeping those times sacred and undisturbed. Make it known what hours of the day you are and aren't available for conversations and consultations.
○ Complete your own work first, then help others.
○ Stick to set working hours, even if you're working from home — in fact, especially if you're working from home.
○ Be honest about what you can and can't do.
○ Ask for help — and accept it — where and when you need it.
○ Make sure to stop for tea and lunch breaks throughout the day.
○ Remove all social media and email apps from your smartphone — less of the smart, more of the phone!
○ Set time aside for social media and email correspondence every day, and stick to it.
○ Allocate a set amount of time for connection and community every day. Use this time to network, catch up with your work friends, ask for input or let off steam. Once the time allocation has been used up, tighten your boundaries by concentrating on your work outputs.

If you do some — or all — of these things, you'll be amazed at how much more energy you have, and how much happier you are.

Can you think of two or three 'tiny' habits that will help you to improve your level of satisfaction in this area and allow your Wheel of Work to give you a smoother ride?

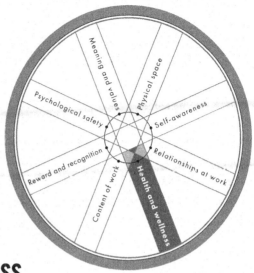

Health and wellness

Work plays an enormous part in our lives and has an enormous impact on our health and happiness; and our health and happiness have an equally important impact on the quality of our work. When we look after our health and wellness, we are able to work better and be more efficient, effective and creative.

While it is incumbent on us to look after our own health in order to have a happy and productive life, there are some work-related health challenges that are important to be aware of in order to prevent or minimise them and the impact they could potentially have on our ability to make work work for us.

Burnout

Burnout is a state of emotional, physical, mental, spiritual and relational exhaustion caused by excessive and prolonged stress. We get burnout when we feel overwhelmed, emotionally drained and unable to meet the constant demands we face.

Global levels of stress and burnout in the workplace have been on the rise for more than a decade, and in 2023 remained at a record high according to American analytics and advisory company Gallup, which conducts an annual report into the state of the global workplace by polling 116 countries.

I believe that we get burnout, not from doing too much, but from doing too much of the things that are wrong for us. It is alarmingly apparent in these strange and stressed post-pandemic times that burnout is also a response to having lived through, and to be living in, a time when so much of what was and is happening to and around us is and has been very, very wrong for us. We have all been stretched too often and too far by events in the last few years, and are all at increased risk of burning out.

There are a number of deep-seated reasons why some of us are more vulnerable to developing burnout than others. Those of us who constantly seek approval and affirmation, who judge ourselves without mercy, who struggle to ask for help, who can't imagine saying 'no', and who have the 'others-centredness' or 'rescuer' genes are very likely to drive ourselves to the point of exhaustion and being completely overwhelmed – and beyond. (You can read more about the link between these in my 2019 book *Recover from Burnout.*)

Burnout comes calling when we are doing not only too many of the wrong things – the things that drain us and make us stressed, angry and resentful – but also not enough of the right things – the things that feed us, restore us and re-energise us. When we have burnout, we feel as though we have nothing left to give and all of our resilience is gone.

Resilience is often described using an analogy of a rubber band, and its ability to bounce back after being stretched. We all have some level of resilience, and we have all bounced back many times after periods of stress and discomfort. As with all things, however, resilience requires some moderation, because when a rubber band is stretched too often or too far, it either snaps or it loses all its bounce. We're the same; when we're stretched (or stretch ourselves) too often, too far or for too long, we'll break or we'll lose all our energy and enthusiasm. That, in a nutshell, is burnout.

When we have burnout, we aren't just physically tired or emotionally delicate. We don't just feel existentially unsure or question all our life choices. (This is why I recommend that my burnout clients try to recover from their burnout before making any drastic life- or career-changing decisions.) It's not only that our brains feel mushy and we struggle to remember things. We aren't merely easily irritated and disappointed. It's all of these things – and more. Burnout impacts *everything*. And the more serious the burnout, the greater the impact.

Burnout is a systemic condition that affects every element and aspect of our lives – it is by no means confined to work. But if we do not address it, and we allow the exhaustion and state of overwhelm to continue, we may begin to lose the enthusiasm and interest that drew us to our jobs in the first place. Burnout can turn work that we valued and found rewarding in every way into something that we resent and recoil from – not because the work has changed but because we have run out of energy and enthusiasm to appreciate it and do it well.

Paradoxically, while burnout makes us and our life force feel diminished, it simultaneously amplifies many of our responses. What might have made us slightly irritable before burnout can send us into a white-hot rage while in burnout. Instead of nibbling a square of chocolate after supper, we demolish a whole bar. Instead of feeling a little bit tired after mental or physical exertion, we feel flattened. Things that used to make us feel a little bit sad become devastating. Tiny sniffles are fast-tracked to bronchitis or pneumonia.

A couple of years after I stopped working at the job from hell, I found myself in the surprising – and surprisingly lovely – position of training police officers. From the very beginning, I was acutely aware that the vast majority of the men and women attending the classes would start their days with coffee, caffeinated energy drinks, chocolate or cigarettes – and often a combination of all of those 'Cs'.

What I suspected then and know definitively now is that they were all in varying stages of burnout. They were beyond exhausted on every level – physical, emotional, mental, spiritual and relational – and were essentially running on the fumes provided by the cortisol-producing fuel they were inhaling. Craving sugar, starchy foods and coffee is always a warning that we're low on energy reserves and needing to kickstart our bodies with caffeine and carbs – the 'bad stuff'.

Some of the other, less visible signs of burnout include headaches, sleep disturbances, digestive ailments, anxiety, impaired concentration, social isolation and withdrawal from relationships, and a feeling of 'what's the point?' Burnout is an 'existential emergency' because the things that used to feel meaningful and important are no longer rewarding or satisfying.

Burnout starts small but, left unchecked, escalates rapidly and can soon make life feel overwhelming and terrifying.

Starting with being in a too-cold environment with horrible pictures on the wall, and moving up to doing work that you are morally and ethically at odds with – and anywhere in between – too much of the wrong thing/s will eventually result in burnout.

When we take on too much, especially too much or too many of the things that make us feel cross, resentful or anxious, we run the risk of developing burnout, not just because we're awash with negative emotions much of the time, but also because we don't have the space to do the things that are right for us, and that restore our energy and enthusiasm for life.

Unless we pay attention to the burnout and intervene to reverse it, it will progress, and the symptoms will worsen. The irritability will become anger. Our quality of sleep will deteriorate into insomnia, which in turn will result in heightened anxiety and worsening physical exhaustion. As a way of trying to make ourselves feel better and treat our growing anxiety and discomfort, we may try to self-medicate by consuming more and more alcohol, prescription and non-prescription drugs, and other substances like energy drinks and chocolates, which may make us feel better in the short term but over time only add to our growing distress and dis-ease.

A not surprising consequence of this progression of burnout symptoms is a breakdown of relationships, an increase in chronic illnesses, and – often – depression. As I warn my clients, if we leave burnout untreated, it can result in one or more of the dreaded three 'Ds': depression, diabetes and divorce.

Burnout and depression are often mistaken for one another. It's extremely important to know the difference, as their treatment is very different.

Both burnout and depression involve a feeling of tiredness to the point of exhaustion; a feeling of not being able to function normally. It's the *quality* of the exhaustion that differs, and it's a very important difference. When we have burnout, we're tired or exhausted *by* life, whereas when we have depression, we're tired or exhausted *of* life.

We get burnout when our life and the way we're living it tires us out, when the choices we make and the actions we take are draining and debilitating. Depression has nothing to do with choices; it's something that happens to us and, when it does, we start to feel tired of our life and as though we don't want to be living it any more.

It's an essential distinction to make because burnout, if caught early enough, can be self-managed and turned around, but depression requires professional help. If you or anyone you know feels tired of life, I urge you to take the necessary steps to get help as quickly as possible. You're not alone – there are plenty of free and subsidised organisations that offer support to people struggling with depression and other mental health challenges.

HOW TO STOP BURNOUT BEHAVIOUR IN ITS TRACKS

We get burnout when we stop looking after ourselves and stop paying attention to our own needs; when we put ourselves in neutral to get through the day without any awareness of our emotions or our desires; when we swallow our irritation with a boss or colleague; and when we light up another cigarette to go with another cup of coffee or gobble down another bar of chocolate instead of making sure we get enough rest and do enough of the things that make us happy and energised.

The simplest and most effective way to stop all of these unhelpful, burnout-generating behaviours is to ask yourself these three questions every day – at least once a day and as often as you need to. I guarantee that these three questions will open a vista of self-knowledge and self-care within minutes!

The three questions are:

1. What am I feeling?
2. Why am I feeling this way?
3. What do I want to do about it?

Here are some examples of answers to these questions:

- **What am I feeling?**

Physically	Emotionally	Mentally	Spiritually	Relationally
Tired Hungry Hot and bothered	Delicate Irritable Resentful Excited Interested	Unable to concentrate Forgetful	What is the point of life? Why is everything so hard?	Disconnected from my friends Irritated with my boss Appreciating my life partner

- **Why am I feeling this way?**

I'm feeling tired and delicate, and I'm struggling to concentrate because I'm not getting enough rest and sleep. I'm hungry and irritable because I worked through lunch and haven't had anything to eat today. I'm hot, bothered and resentful because my boss has asked me to take the minutes in the meeting again and never seems to ask my male colleague. It adds extra work to my already too-busy day, and makes me cross that I'm expected to do it because I'm a woman.

- **What do I want to do about it?**

I'm going to go to bed and be asleep by 10pm every night so that I can get enough rest and do better at work. I'm going to set an alarm on my phone to remind me when it's time to step away from my computer and have a healthy lunch. I'm going to speak to my colleague, who is also a friend, and ask for his support in the next meeting by speaking up and saying that he will take the notes in that meeting so that I can concentrate on my work.

George was so burned out when he came to me for coaching that he was on the verge of handing in his resignation. He was amazingly successful at a job that he valued, and where he was highly valued, but he was running on the very few fumes he had left in his tank. He managed multiple teams, was running up to seven projects at a time and travelled a lot – all of which he did well and enjoyed in and of themselves, although they were all pretty exhausting.

The problem was that the incredibly long hours he was working, and the number of nights he was away from home, meant that he was missing out on spending time with his family and attending his kids' school plays and sports events – the things that restored and generated energy for him. He didn't have the time and space to replenish all the energy he was expending at work. His energy levels were becoming more and more depleted, and he was feeling more and more desperate.

We embarked on the burnout rapid-response protocol that I've developed to support people like George. I helped him to identify:
- *What he could say 'no' to.*
- *What he could ask for help with.*
- *How he could get more rest.*
- *How he could generate energy to replenish his stores.*

The most awful thing about burnout is that the harder we try, the less effective we feel, which made it hard for George to say 'no' to anything with a clear conscience. But he did manage to start saying 'no' to staying at work past 5pm. This meant that, when he wasn't travelling, he could be home in time to have dinner with his family, spend time with his children and catch up with his wife. After the evening meal where everyone could tell their stories and share their days, leaving him feeling more energised and enthusiastic, George allowed himself to work for another couple of hours.

Interestingly, after only a couple of weeks, he didn't need to work at home after dinner because his replenishing energy was allowing him to get more done during the working day, as was his increasing ability to delegate (which is a way of asking for help).

The more rested and replenished George felt, the less anxious he was and the easier it became for him to ask his very competent and more willing team members to take on additional responsibilities – including much of the travel –

which they willingly and ably did. The teams became more cohesive, the projects ran more smoothly, and the results spoke for themselves.

By addressing his own burnout, George built up his staff and created an environment that lent itself to preventing burnout by creating the space for everyone to spend their energy wisely and well.

Unfortunately, the Georges of the world are plentiful – most of my burnout clients come to me when they're burned out to a crisp and it's almost unthinkable to them that they will ever feel any better. This is the reason my burnout coaching focus has moved from recovery only to prevention as well.

Preventing and recovering from burnout – and ensuring that we stay recovered – requires fundamental and far-reaching changes to how we live our lives. You will have a better chance of success if you start small and are consistent.

Every day, consider the burnout rapid-response protocol questions:
- What can you say 'no' to?
- What can you ask for help with?
- How can you get more rest?
- How can you generate energy to replenish your stores?

For example, you could say 'no' to staying up late, or that seventh cup of coffee, or going to a social event you hate the idea of. You could ask for help with feedback on a draft report or for an instruction to be explained again. You could get more sleep and rest by going to bed earlier, by napping for 15 minutes instead of scrolling through social media, or by stepping away from all technology at least an hour before bed so that when you turn in, your brain will be relaxed enough to go to sleep. And you can replenish your energy stores by doing things that you love, seeing people who make you happy, eating nourishing meals, and moving your body in the fresh air.

It sounds simple but be warned: simple does not necessarily mean easy! These habits are often hard to adopt – not because they're complicated, but because they go against our instincts of wanting to be seen to be strong and competent, of wanting to please everybody, and of wanting to work hard and push ourselves to achieve and succeed.

Burnout results when we spend too much time and attention on things that drain us and our energy levels, and not enough time and attention on the things that restore or generate more energy for us.

If I were to ask you how much money you have available in your bank account right now, I'm sure you would have a pretty good idea what is (or isn't) there, what you can expect to come in, and what you can expect to go out. Most of us keep a mental running tab of our bank balance and have a good sense of whether or not we can afford that meal out this evening, or those new shoes now, or if we need to save up for a couple of months before we can splash out.

But we don't do the same with our energy, even though, just like money, it's a finite resource. We pay little or no heed to our vitality balance, spending our energy with abandon until we use up all our reserves and have nothing left in our energy account.

Ernest Hemingway famously had one of his characters (in his 1926 novel *The Sun Also Rises*) explain that his bankruptcy had happened 'gradually, then suddenly', and running out of energy (or developing burnout) is exactly the same. With money, we overspend a little, then a little more, then a little more, until we're so far into overdraft and our credit-card bills are so high that we have no more wiggle room. With energy, we exert ourselves too much, then stretch ourselves a little further, then extend ourselves a little more, until we're so far into an energy deficit that we're exhausted and overwhelmed, and have no more energy or enthusiasm to do what we need to do.

When we've reached the point of being energetically bankrupt, and we have nothing left to give, then we may start to think that our work is untenable, when in fact it is often how we think about and manage our energy that is the problem.

If we are to make work work for us, we need to pay as much attention to our energy-flow as we do to our cashflow. We need to identify what we're doing that's using up our energy, and what we're doing, or can do, to restore and generate energy for ourselves – both at work and outside of it.

Just like with our bank accounts, we need to ensure that at the very least we are breaking even on our energy income and expenditure; and if we generate more energy than we spend, we can create some savings. The more we save, the more energy reserves we will have to draw on in an emergency – when we have to pull an all-nighter to complete a report, for instance.

It is useful to draw up an energy-balance sheet to help us keep an eye on our energy incomings and outgoings. The energy-balance sheet has three columns: things that drain our energy, things that restore our energy (bringing us back to a place of neutral rest), and things that actively generate energy for us.

To create your own energy balance sheet, draw up a table with three columns, headed 'Energy drainers', 'Energy restorers' and 'Energy generators'. You're going to fill the columns with all the things that you can think of that drain, restore and generate your energy. You don't have to restrict yourself to work-related items; in fact, it's good to think of as many non-work-related energy restorers and generators as you can. The three questions 'What am I feeling?', 'Why am I feeling this way?' and 'What do I want to do about it?' are a very good way to identify the things that drain, restore and generate energy for you.

First, write down your energy drainers – the things that make you feel exhausted, unmotivated, uncomfortable, angry, helpless, anxious, insecure, uncertain, unable to look after yourself properly, etc. (The list you drew up on page 12, of those things that are not working for you at work, will probably include many things that drain your energy.)

Now, fill in your energy restorers – the things that help you to relax, and feel calm and un-stressed.

Finally, fill in our energy generators – those things that make you feel happy, invigorated, energised, optimistic, competent and powerful.

Think about how you can use the items in the 'restorers' and 'generators' columns to offset the items in the 'drainers' column. Some may have an obvious link, like conducting boring tasks with entertaining people or while listening to music, while others will not have such a clear correlation – you may have to go for a swim after work and have an early night to balance out an energy-draining day. Think about how you can do more of what you enjoy and feels good to you, and if there is anything you can do to protect yourself from energy drainers, or expose yourself to fewer of them.

Here's an example of my energy-balance sheet:

Energy drains	Energy restorers	Energy generators
Tax returns Admin Workshops on Zoom Being bored Going to a shopping mall	Reading Having a proper lunch break outside Walking Listening to podcasts Painting and drawing	Connecting with friends Coaching Training Writing In-person workshops Aqua pilates Laughing

In a magical universe, I would never have to do admin or tax returns, and I would be able to fly all over the world and never have to offer another workshop on Zoom. Sadly, in the universe I – and you – inhabit, many of the tasks that use up my energy are non-negotiable.

Happily, there are more things that restore and generate energy for me, so it's easy for me to offset the expenditure against the income. I can, for instance, make sure to meet a friend for a walk or lunch every day, and set up my diary so that I have at least the same number of coaching and in-person workshops as I do Zoom workshops and admin every day.

As long as I remain mindful and ensure that I'm doing enough of the things in columns two and three, I will always have enough energy to deal with the things in column one. The same will be true for you.

Work starts working for us as soon as we have enough energy and enthusiasm to do what needs to be done to remove and improve the things that aren't working for us.

Compassion fatigue

As much as I know and believe that we can prevent and recover from burnout by spending our energy mindfully and wisely, and ensuring we do enough of the things that are good for us to balance the things that aren't, I also know that there are some situations that are immune to all the wellness hacks and self-awareness techniques, and can lead us to develop a very particular kind of exhaustion called compassion fatigue.

'I need to deal with my irritation, impatience and lack of excitement about life.' This is how Reggie described why he had come to me for coaching. He went on to explain that he'd been drinking too much coffee in the daytime, too much wine in the evenings and not enough water ever. He also was exercising too little, eating badly and not sleeping well. His concentration was a shadow of its former glory and his productivity reflected this.

But perhaps the most troubling symptom of his exhaustion was the not-so-gradual erosion of his empathy. Reggie had always been known as a very compassionate and patient person, always going the extra mile to help people any way he could. 'Now, I have no time or patience for anyone. If a staff member asks for help, I feel irritated. If my manager asks for my input on something, I seethe while I'm doing it. If my wife asks me to make supper, I bang and crash the pots and pans to show how cross I feel to be asked.'

I asked Reggie what he thought was contributing to the way he was feeling, and he was flummoxed. 'That's what I find so confusing – and even more irritating!' he said. 'My work is going exceptionally well. I'm travelling much less, so I have a better work-life balance. I'm in the sweet spot of being experienced enough to do my work easily, while still being stimulated and excited by it. I'm happy with where I am at work and on my pay scale. My relationship with my wife is great. I love my children. I have time and money to spend on cycling and going on nice holidays. It just makes no sense at all that I'm feeling this way!'

Was there anything in his life that was troubling or challenging him, I wondered? Anything that had changed recently or that he felt upset by?

After much dithering, Reggie admitted that, as awful as it made him feel to say it, he was finding the fact that his ageing and ailing father had recently moved in with him and his family very difficult. 'I love my dad and I feel terrible to say this out loud, but he has started to drive me mad. As soon as any of the family get home, he expects them to go and have a cup of tea with him and sit and listen to his stories for hours. When we explain that the kids have homework, or we have things that we need to catch up on, he sulks. He doesn't like the meals we eat and complains that they're too spicy or too salty or not tasty enough... there's always something wrong. If we watch a movie together as family, he keeps up a running commentary about how silly or loud or violent or stupid it is. We're too anxious to invite friends around for a meal because we know that if he eats with us, he'll monopolise the conversation, but if we ask him to eat in his room, we'll never hear the end of how we don't want him there...' Once Reggie got started, it was like a runaway train!

I managed to interject with the observation that it sounded a lot like Reggie was experiencing compassion fatigue, a condition that's often described as 'the cost of caring' because it's a response to the ongoing stress of caring for or about others. When we have compassion fatigue, I explained, we feel emotionally, physically and/or spiritually exhausted as a result of caring for or about people, particularly people in significant emotional pain and/or physical distress.

'Yes! That's exactly what I'm going through. I love my dad, I really do, and I'm so pleased to be able to have him in our home, but he's always there, always demanding attention, always talking about his aches and pains, always needing something or other. I feel awful when I get impatient with him because I know he's sore and sad – he misses my mother terribly – but sometimes he just pushes us too far, and I get impatient with him and then I feel bad for being impatient. It's all horrible.'

Once Reggie was able to see that his exhaustion and irritation were a result of compassion fatigue, he was able to be more mindful about taking care of himself and seeking out support and help. He and his wife identified members of the extended family who could take turns to come and visit the old man. They soon had a roster of visitors, which meant that Reggie's father had someone to have tea with and talk to every day of the week, cheering him up and stimulating him. It also meant that at supper time he had more of an appetite and more to contribute to the conversation. His complaining reduced and everyone in the immediate and extended family liked spending more time with him.

By decreasing the amount of time he spent with his dad, Reggie increased the satisfaction that both of them experienced when they were together.

Compassion fatigue looks and feels a lot like burnout, but, as Reggie demonstrated, perhaps the most distressing aspect of compassion fatigue is a sense of depersonalisation and a diminished ability to empathise with or feel compassion for others.

For people who are naturally caring and kind and want to help others, developing compassion fatigue can mean an alarming loss of this innate kindheartedness and desire to help make things better for those around us. Despite – or perhaps because of – the fact that our lives or our work may demand us to be sensitive to the needs of others, when we have compassion fatigue, we feel a sense of removal from the pain and suffering we're exposed to, a numbness towards or even an impatience with people we would ordinarily want to help. It's a very real, and very horrible, consequence of being emotionally and empathically overwhelmed, and is often the aspect of compassion fatigue that people who experience it find most upsetting – far more worrying than the other symptoms, which are almost identical to those of burnout.

Any profession or pastime that requires us to show others compassion or empathy on an ongoing basis bears the risk of compassion fatigue. Empathy is the feeling that you understand and share another person's experiences and emotions, or have the ability to share someone else's feelings. It is often our empathy that makes us both extremely good workers and sensitive and supportive co-workers, and extremely sensitive and vulnerable to emotion overload – and compassion fatigue.

Compassion fatigue is an accepted occupational hazard of the 'caring' professions (healthcare workers, educators, therapists, coaches) but it is becoming more common generally. I see teachers, journalists and HR managers suffering from compassion fatigue. I also see people like Reggie, who have the responsibility of caring for old, infirm and/or chronically ill family members, with compassion fatigue. And, increasingly, there's a recognition that being exposed – through the media and in real life – to the enormous suffering and injustices that we see around us every day is on its own enough to give the more sensitive among us compassion fatigue.

Studies have shown that the more compassionate and empathic the person, the greater their risk of developing compassion fatigue. So, the better those of us who are paid to care are at our jobs, the more vulnerable we are to compassion fatigue and burnout.

Some of us take on the helping role at work, even when it isn't our core business. We do this when we're motivated by a desire (and sometimes an expectation) to provide support and care for others. We want to help them to be happy, reach their dreams, and find happiness and fulfilment. And, often, we're hoping to do the same for ourselves in the process.

Unfortunately, for many of us, our desire to help others sometimes overrides our ability to help ourselves. In our enthusiasm to heal others, we can end up harming ourselves by wearing away at our energy and empathy until we're left with nothing to give.

The trouble with compassion fatigue is that, as with burnout, it creeps up on us so stealthily and feels like such a logical progression of our experiences, that many people who experience compassion fatigue aren't aware of it until it's full-blown.

HOW TO COMBAT COMPASSION FATIGUE

Whether you have compassion fatigue as a result of a personal situation or because your profession demands you be endlessly empathic, the steps I suggest for overcoming and preventing compassion fatigue are the same. As we say in coaching, how you do anything is how you do everything, and if we can introduce some habits for our health and wellbeing, we can ensure that, like Reggie, we remain not only effective and efficient, but also burnout- and compassion fatigue-free.

Talk about it

We carry all our difficult emotions with us, and unless we find a safe place to put those feelings, we're in grave danger of developing compassion fatigue and/or burnout. We all need to have a safe space to put down or make sense of what's going on inside of us: our reactions to a difficult conversation, the way we feel after we've witnessed an injustice, the anxiety we experience in anticipation of a big presentation. The more we can share our worries in a safe and trustworthy space, the more effective we'll be able to be at work.

It's also important to find someone we can tell about our victories – our promotions, our successes, our positive feedback. Just as a trouble shared is a trouble halved, so a joy shared is a joy doubled.

There may be someone at work or at home to whom you can download your days, or you may need to find yourself a therapist or a coach to help you sort through your emotions. If you aren't able to speak to a person, then 'writing yourself well' in a journal is an excellent option. Whoever or whatever avenue you choose, make working through your experiences a regular non-negotiable.

Look after yourself

Many who are drawn to caring for others are what I call 'others-centred'. This means that we tend to put other people first – at the centre of our worlds – and ourselves last. People who are others-centred are particularly prone to compassion fatigue and burnout because they're so busy looking after everyone else that they forget to look after themselves.

We need to take self-care seriously to enable us to take care of others.

If you can take care of yourself through paying attention to diet, rest, exercise, play, journalling, meditating, creating, learning and talking about your struggles, then you will be able to continue to do the work that's meaningful and rewarding to you without burning out.

Spend your energy wisely and give yourself some breaks

Pay attention to your energy levels and be sure that you don't overload yourself by committing to more than you can comfortably handle.

Make sure that you're not only limiting the number of 'wrong things' you're doing, but that you're doing enough of the 'right things' to fill your energy account. All work and no play not only makes us dull, it makes us tired and overwhelmed too. It's essential that we schedule in proper downtime to rest and recuperate.

We all have different energy and stamina levels, and we all do different work that requires different resources in the form of time, energy and enthusiasm. You need to work out what is the best way that you can spend your time and energy in order to be the best at what you do.

Be you

The temptation to 'compare and despair' can be overwhelming. We look at other people and calculate how much money they're making, imagine how successful they are, wonder at how patient and kind they are with their parents – never mind that the people we're comparing ourselves to have totally different lives, responsibilities, ecosystems, personalities, strengths and weaknesses to our own. Then we put ourselves under pressure to achieve the same – even if those achievements are figments of our imagination.

One of the best ways to guard against compassion fatigue and burnout is to be yourself. Remember yourself and your own interests, keep learning, keep growing, and use your strengths and superpowers for good – yours and everyone else's.

Have a healthy ecosystem

You're at greater risk of developing compassion fatigue and burnout – and all sorts of other ailments, both physical and emotional – if you have toxic and draining relationships in your personal life. If you don't look after your physical health, you're at greater risk of developing compassion fatigue. If you don't have a safe outlet for your fears and anxieties, you're at greater risk of developing compassion fatigue. If you aren't getting enough sleep, exercising enough or eating enough healthy food, you're in danger of exacerbating the burnout or compassion fatigue you may already have.

In order to be healthy and well, and as productive and happy at work as we can possibly be, it's important that we have a healthy and supportive ecosystem (see page 159 for more about this).

Making sense of all the information about burnout and compassion fatigue can feel confusing and overwhelming – especially for those who have burnout and compassion fatigue! To make it easier to assess if you're experiencing either or both, I developed the questionnaire below. (Note that this is not a diagnostic measurement and should not be used in place of a professional assessment – please refer to your healthcare provider for professional input.)

Burnout and compassion fatigue quick assessment tool

Things to consider	Yes	No
I find myself worried about personal stresses when I am at work		
My relationships at home are strained		
I am spending less time with my family/friends than I would like		
I am feeling less supported and understood by colleagues than I am used to		
I am easily drained — even by small changes and events		
It is taking me longer to recover from hearing about or experiencing crime, violence or trauma		
I am deeply affected by the stresses of the people I work with		
I am less patient with colleagues than usual		
I have lower expectations of everyone (especially the people I work with) than usual		
I no longer feel hopeful and optimistic about the future		
I feel vulnerable all the time		
I feel overwhelmed by everything I have on my plate		
I am having difficulty sleeping and/or wake up feeling tired and unrefreshed		
I am craving more sweets, carbohydrates and/or caffeine than usual		
It feels as though my brain is foggy and working more slowly than usual		
I am more irritable and emotional than usual		
My work no longer feels as meaningful as it used to		
It is hard to remember why I decided to do this work		
I am experiencing some health issues (dizziness, nausea, stomach complaints, headaches, loss of appetite, high blood pressure, anxiety)		

Count the number of ticks you have in the 'yes' column:

0-5: You're in pretty good shape. Keep it up by continuing to look after yourself and your energy.

6-10: You're sneaking up to burnout or compassion fatigue. See where you can start asking for help, saying 'no', and ensuring you spend your energy wisely.

11-15: You have burnout or compassion fatigue. You need to pay serious attention to how you're showing up for yourself to avoid a full-blown health crisis.

16+: You're in the danger zone. Seek urgent help to ensure that you recover from your burnout or compassion fatigue before it progresses to more serious health challenges.

Perimenopause and menopause

Shireen was finally in the management role she had worked towards her whole professional life. She had overcome the slew of the economic, educational and social challenges that many women are faced with along the way. With sheer determination and a lot of hard work, she had reached the position she'd been aiming for since she left school. Her kids were grown, her marriage was reaping the rewards of being financially stable and having some time and space to breathe, and she had a supportive social circle. All seemed to be right in her world.

And then the steamy, foggy red mist of impending menopause descended. Almost overnight, Shireen found herself forgetting things – not just her login details or why she had walked into a room, but career-impacting things like the names of her colleagues and clients (and the name of the woman who brought her tea every day, which was far more upsetting).

Shireen found herself getting hot and bothered, and unable to think clearly and coolly, numerous times a day as she endured stifling hot flushes. While addressing her colleagues, she would be in full articulate flow when her brain would screech to a halt, and she would hold up a hand to signify that she needed some time to find the words she knew were there, but just couldn't connect with.

'I'll be sitting in a meeting, fully engaged with the discussions, when I start to feel it: a hot, prickly wave of discomfort that starts in my feet and moves up through my whole body. It makes me feel so panicky and claustrophobic that I lose all my focus on what is going on around me, and become totally engrossed with what it feels like inside me. I can't think clearly, the points I want to make are lost, and all my attention is on how hot, sweaty and uncomfortable I feel. It can last anything from one to five minutes – long enough to take me out of the engagement and lose the opportunity to make any meaningful contribution to that agenda item. It makes we want to curl up into a ball and howl.'

Because of her increased anxiety and the relentless hot flushes, Shireen wasn't getting enough sleep, was putting on weight, and was becoming increasingly irritable and stressed. 'A hot mess' is how she described herself to me.

'It's so unfair! I'm finally in a position where I can and should be making a real difference, and instead of being on top of my game, I feel like a fraud,' she said as she wept into a handful of squishy tissues. 'Sometimes it all feels too hard, and I'm starting to think maybe it would be best if I just resigned and stayed home where I can surrender to my hot flushes and amnesia in peace.'

Put simply, menopause is the time that marks the end of a woman's menstrual cycle; you're considered to be in menopause when you've gone 12 months without a period.

The four to eight (and sometimes longer) years leading up to this are called perimenopause, and are a period of fluctuating hormones that lead to a whole lot of symptoms – just a few of which have a direct impact on our ability to do our work. These include hot flushes and night sweats, sleep disturbance, forgetfulness, depression, anxiety and mood swings.

These, and other features of this time in a woman's life, can be very unsettling and feel deeply unjust. Every woman who reaches a position of leadership and management has had to make compromises – a varied multitude – that often even they aren't aware of all of them. And to be faced with what often feels like an organic, untameable beast that is rampaging on the inside, determined to undermine us at every turn, feels unfair in the extreme.

Just as more mature women are finally being seen for what we bring to the conference table rather than what we are wearing to it, our hormones conspire to make us feel messy, inarticulate and irritable. It feels as though our bodies and our emotions are a foreign country that's waging a war against us. Often, getting out of bed and going in to work feels like an extremely high and steep hill to climb.

Much has been written about women leaving the workforce because of burnout and the recognition of the need for better balance, but I believe that one of the reasons that isn't being talked about is that many menopausal women no longer have the energy or inclination to continue to fight the battles they've had to engage with their whole careers. There's no more patience for the micro-aggressions and undermining that they may have put up with for decades. There's no more energy for the sexism, the eye-rolling, the mansplaining. And there's not enough resilience to withstand the ignorance and lack of information about menopause and what it means for the people experiencing it.

We don't roll our eyes and make discouraging noises to each other when a team member has to put on their spectacles in order to read the agenda points, but we do when a female colleague's glasses mist up during a hot flush, or when she needs to take a few extra seconds to connect with the word she wants to use to make a point.

The management and leadership publication *Harvard Business Review* published an article in 2022 on this very subject. To improve the writer's understanding (and ours) of the impact of hot flushes (or hot flashes, as the American writer, Alicia Grandey, a professor of industrial-organisational psychology, calls them) in the workplace, Grandey conducted a series of studies that explored the stereotypes associated with menopause, how menopause impacts on women's careers, and how men and women can engage with menopause in order to overcome any bias.

She found that people perceived menopausal women to be less confident and less emotionally stable – in other words, less effective leaders – than women who weren't menopausal. Interestingly, however, when women spoke openly and honestly about experiencing symptoms related to menopause – 'I'm okay, it's just that menopausal time of life' – they were seen as more confident, stable leaders than women who didn't refer to their menopause experience.

As Grandey concluded, while the study showed that there were clear negative stereotypes associated with being menopausal, 'the act of disclosing your own menopausal status conveys confidence and stability, essentially cancelling out the negative biases that people would otherwise hold'. In other words, it seems that the more we take the topic offline and confine its engagement to those who are experiencing it, the more mystical and secretive we make it – and the more we make women open to shaming and sidelining.

Sadly, what support there is in the workplace for the symptoms and effects that menopause has on women in their professional prime is confined to those who understand the issue. It's great that companies are starting to offer support and information to women who are in this phase of our lives, but we need to stop othering women in general – and menopausal women in particular – and make it a topic of conversation and understanding for all of us.

Menopause isn't and shouldn't be a dirty, shameful secret. It is a natural progression of our maturing process – as natural and predictable as our hair greying and our eyesight dimming. We don't have separate support groups for people who have recently been prescribed reading glasses, or for staff members who dye their hair, why do we offer behind-the-door help to women in menopause?

Grandey's research shows that acknowledging hot flushes when they happen and 'simply stating – without embarrassment or shame – that they are due to menopause is an effective way to demonstrate self-confidence and leadership potential'. And, of course, each time someone talks openly about menopause, they normalise the experience and make it easier for others to follow suit.

> *Shireen and I discussed the Grandey article, and she decided to be more open about the wringer her body was putting her through. When she had a hot flush, she calmly took off her glasses to wipe them and said, 'Hot flush time,' while smiling and shaking her head. When she struggled to think of a word she said, 'It will come to me, it's just making its way through the hormone traffic.' By doing this, Shireen felt less anxious, and the people around her became more accepting and patient. She also reported back to me that many of her women colleagues expressed their appreciation of her normalising menopause and educating the organisation – including many of the women in it – about it.*

If we're to allow menopausal women to take their rightful place as skilled leaders with huge amounts of knowledge and experience to share, we need to overcome the bias against them. We need to build workplace cultures that encourage talking about menopause and normalising it, just as we do with all other aspects of maturing.

WHAT TO DO IF YOU THINK YOU'RE IN MENOPAUSE

- Ask for help. Go to your GP or gynae to look at treatment options. Science is on our side, and there are many options to treat both the symptoms and the hormonal causes of menopause.
- Speak up. Despite being taught to hide what are bodies are up to, we need

to talk out. Make menopause mainstream. Mention when you're having a hot flush or a brain-freeze moment. Stop protecting everyone (mostly men) from the reality of menopause. The more we speak about it, the more we can normalise it and bring it (and ourselves) out of hiding.

- Identify what support you (and your peers) need to make your work work better for you – and ask for it. These may be practical (your own air-conditioner, a desk at a window that opens, being allowed to work from home on bad days), medical (time off for doctor's visits, access to subsidised treatments), or emotional (the space to be honest about what you're experiencing without feeling judged or mocked).

WHAT TO DO IF YOU WORK WITH OR FOR SOMEONE EXPERIENCING MENOPAUSE

- Read up on menopause so you understand what your colleague may be going through. We can't be supportive about something we don't understand.
- Be accommodating about things like air-conditioning and access to windows.
- Practise patience and empathy. If a colleague is scrabbling for words or is obviously in the grip of a hot flush, resist the temptation to be 'helpful' and let them tell you what, if anything, they need from you.
- Remember that menopause is as natural and predictable as other signs of ageing; it's nothing to be scared of or uncomfortable about.

There are many, many aspects of health and wellness that are not covered in this chapter. Burnout, compassion fatigue, energy management and menopause are discussed here because they're so topical and such prevalent issues at this time, and because the strategies presented to deal with each of them can be as effective and applicable to other health concerns.

Can you think of two or three 'tiny' habits that will help you to improve your level of satisfaction in this area and allow your Wheel of Work to give you a smoother ride?

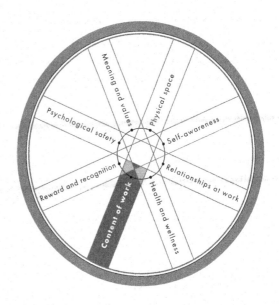

Content of work

There are many aspects to our work that contribute to our job satisfaction or lack thereof. What often gets overlooked in the noise generated by community and culture and conditions and compensation is the actual content of the work – the reason we chose to embark on that career. Whether it's balancing books, designing buildings, conducting and collating research or shaping young minds, whatever career we choose requires us to spend a substantial amount of time on the nuts and bolts of our chosen contribution to the world of work.

It's unlikely that we will feel completely in tune and happy with all of the content of our work every single day. In all probability, we'll go through patches of feeling stressed, bored, anxious, avoidant or alienated, or have some or other difficult response when we sit down at our desk. Understanding and working with these responses is key to making work work for us.

Stimulation and boredom

One of the many reasons we choose to work is because of the stimulation that's promised by going out and doing a job every day. We're stimulated in different ways and to different degrees by the work we do and by the environment we work in. While some people may prefer to have a job that's predictable and without drama, for example, others may wither without the stimulation of pressure and excitement.

If we're lucky, stimulation is predominantly positive. We love the content of our work, and we find the assignments and projects we're allocated interesting and creatively exciting. We're stretched to learn and grow. We enjoy the people and teams we work with. We have encounters and exposure to places that feed us and help us to expand our experience of the world in general and our world in particular.

But most jobs can't sustain positive stimulation all the time, and there will inevitably be spells of relative peace and quiet from time to time. These periods of calm allow for introspection and learning – and appreciation for the next bout of exhilaration. When there aren't enough times for reflection and recovery, however, work can start to feel overstimulating.

Overstimulation
When we are in a prolonged state of overstimulation or in an environment that stimulates us in ways that are odds with our own value system, we shift into survival mode just to get through the days and their demands. And if the demands do not end or alleviate, the physical and emotional stresses of constantly being on high alert will almost inevitably result in burnout.

By the same token, when there are not enough periods of downtime, too much of a good thing can turn bad. If we're constantly having thrilling or adrenaline-charged experiences and 'positive' pressure, we can become almost addicted to the drama and seek out more and more excitement – which can result in our becoming overstimulated, and eventually snapping like an overworked rubber band.

Helen was one of my clients who experienced relentless stimulation. Her to-do lists never seemed to get any shorter, and each item she managed to achieve and cross off was immediately replaced by one or two more tasks. And, for her, there was no space to coast through a meeting and catch up on some emails while other people were talking – she felt she had to be fully present and engaged, and giving direction in every forum of which she was part.

She loved her work and found it interesting and challenging but the constant feeling of being pulled in too many directions was becoming fragmenting and frightening. She told me she didn't even have time to catch up on personal conversations while in the car because she had to catch up on staff calls; every minute of her too-long working day (and many before and after) was taken up with competing work demands. She was so busy and so stressed that she couldn't see the wood for the trees. She had become frantic and had forgotten how to look after herself.

By the time she came to see me, she was a burned-out wreck. She wasn't eating. She wasn't sleeping. She couldn't shake a cold that had been lingering for months. Her family and friends were cross with her for neglecting them.

She had allowed herself to be stretched too far and for too long.

When I suggested that she may want to think about asking for help, taking a break, or at the very least slowing down a bit, Helen was horrified. 'I've worked my butt off to get to where I am: listened to, taken seriously, and having some influence. I can't mess with that now by showing weakness. And, anyway, I love my work and it makes me feel good to be doing so well at it.'

Helen continued to push herself, and a couple of months after we'd had that conversation, she experienced a terrifying panic attack that was so bad she landed up in the emergency room. The doctor who attended to her diagnosed extreme stress and booked her off work for three months. The decision to slow down and accept help had been made for her.

After three months of rest and recuperation, her body and her mind had calmed down enough for her to start making different, better choices for herself when she returned to work. She realised that nothing terrible would happen to her career if she delegated more responsibilities and worked shorter hours, but something terrible may happen to her health and personal life if she didn't.

The thing about the kind of stimulation that Helen was experiencing is that it can be seductive. There's nothing like the high we get when we're feeling effective, proficient and – most captivating – indispensable. This is true for everyone, but for many people – often women – who've had to fight through multiple social and professional barriers to get to positions of worth and influence, it can be very hard to moderate work demands and create a sustainable way of managing stress and stimulation. But if (when) we don't pay attention, we become worn out, strung out and burned out – a very unsustainable approach to our career path.

Negative stimulation

When we're fearful, experiencing or witnessing conflict, stressed or anxious because we feel out of our depth or unable to perform the way we're expected to, we are experiencing negative stimulation. A horrible boss who delights in shaming or humiliating their staff is a negative stimulation. A toxic work environment that makes you feel scared or ill to be in is a whole lot of negative stimulation. Pressure to behave in a certain way or produce something that feels at odds with our personal ethics or value system is negative stimulation.

Unfortunately, we're living and working in a time when ethics have become a little elastic. I wish I could say that I have had no, or even only a couple of, clients who have experienced the burden of being expected to conduct themselves in an inappropriate or unethical manner. Sadly, this is not the case.

One person in particular springs to mind. He was the finance manager in an office that was led by a person of – to put it politely – dubious morals, who in turn had been appointed by a person of even more dubious morals. My client, let's call him John, found himself under increasing pressure to give contracts to service providers who were obviously the least qualified and most expensive applicants. Every time he said 'no' to the pressure to make these appointments, quoting the company's financial policies as he did so, he faced greater resistance and hostility. At first, he was undermined in meetings, then he wasn't invited to meetings. Then he started to receive veiled and then blatant threats about what would happen to him and his family if he didn't appoint 'preferred' candidates.

John struggled valiantly to do his job properly and well, but in the end it got too stressful for him, and his aversion to his boss and to the workplace became too strong a negative stimulus for him to override. He left for a job in a more honourable organisation, where he felt safer and was able to do his work unhindered. But he took with him an enormous burden of guilt that he hadn't been able to put a stop to the toxic practices that were now unhindered in his previous workplace.

Sometimes it isn't possible to remove or improve what isn't working for us in our work environment, and the only way we can better our working life is to extricate ourselves from a hostile environment. I don't say this lightly as I know that jobs aren't always easy to find, and I do believe that we have a large role to play in our experience of work, but when an organisation is too toxic, or is unethical, it's best to improve our experience by removing ourselves from the environment completely.

Boredom
Having to endure the other end of the stimulation spectrum for too long can be just as excruciating; in many ways as challenging as overstimulation or negative stimulation is the opposite extreme, which is not enough or no stimulation.

We all benefit from the downtime that allows us to gather our resources for the next stretch of excitement. However, when these downtimes come around more and more often or for longer stretches, some of us may start to find our work understimulating, maybe even boring.

Boredom is one of the most common reasons my clients give for wanting to leave their jobs. They feel they aren't learning or growing, and could do the work they do on automatic pilot – in fact, many of them do. For people who are bored at their job, work is a place to go to pass the time before they can go home and, at the end of the month, get their paycheque. And the awful thing about boredom is that the more bored we are, the slower time passes.

Boredom isn't about not having enough to do so much as it about not being sufficiently challenged and stimulated while doing it.

Studies on boredom and alienation from work reveal that boredom and disengagement stem from a combination of a lack of control or choice over what we do and how we do it, unchallenging tasks, a lack of recognition of our efforts, and doing things that we do not feel are meaningful or important. There's no doubt that ongoing boredom impacts negatively on us – we become stressed, unproductive and uncreative, and begin to feel bad about our work and ourselves.

Because we spend so much of our time working, being bored can lead to reduced happiness, motivation and engagement in all areas of life, which can ultimately lead to burnout, depression and/or chronic illnesses.

For many people, being understimulated or bored takes as much of a toll on their health and happiness as being overstimulated or stressed does. A lack of challenge, growth and meaning can wear a person and their enthusiasm for the job right down.

Ideally, we want to be kept busy doing work that's interesting and engaging. When we have too much repetition and not enough variety, we start to feel like factory workers on a production line – doing the same thing over and over again, and never feeling a part of the big picture of what's being created.

While there will inevitably be some aspects of every job that are less than thrilling, you don't have to resign yourself to being bored at work forever. There are a number of things you can do to perk things up a bit.

The goal is to be doing less of the things that bore you and more of the things that excite you. Perhaps you can speak to your manager about being assigned new and different work that will be more of a challenge.

You can also make the drudge work feel less soul-destroying by mindfully managing it. For example, you could allocate an hour a day to doing the boring bits of your job – and be disciplined about getting as much done in that hour as you can! Then reward yourself with something you enjoy once you've completed your hour – a cup of coffee, a few minutes on your social media accounts, catching up with a colleague... If it's possible, try to schedule the boring hour before a natural deadline like a staff meeting or the end of the day, so that you will have to stop the task and get up and walk away from your desk in order to go to the meeting or home.

They say misery loves company – and so does boredom. Is it possible to do the boring bits in company? You could do this either by setting up a communal workstation with colleagues, or by taking yourself off to a coffee shop or a busy place that will allow you to get some external stimulation while you do your boring work.

You could ask about being given the opportunity to learn – either by shadowing a colleague or by registering for a more formal education programme. It's always useful, when making such a request, to go to your manager with as much information as possible. Know what you want to study and why, how your gaining competence in this field will benefit your work and the company more broadly, and what options for the learning are available – including costing and how much time your classes will take up. If your employer isn't able to support you with the course fees, there are a number of useful and well-recognised online learning platforms that offer very affordable courses and degrees.

Even though it may not feel like it, boredom is an invitation to think differently about the things that are boring you, and to come up with some creative solutions that feel more interesting. If you regard your boredom as an opportunity for growth, you'll be taking another step forward in making work work for you.

As Goldilocks taught us, we don't want our stimulation porridge to be too hot or too cold, we want it to be just right. To find that middle ground, we need to take charge of the levels and kinds of stimulation we experience at work.

To help you find a stimulation balance that suits you, ask yourself:
- In what way is your work positively stimulating for you? What makes you feel happy, invigorated, energised, optimistic, competent, powerful, etc?
- What can you do to ensure that you experience the right amount of positive stimulation for you? How can you do enough – but not too much – of what you enjoy and feels good to you?
- In what way is work negatively stimulating for you? What makes you feel uncomfortable, angry, helpless, anxious, insecure, uncertain, overstimulated, unable to look after yourself properly, etc?
- What can you do to try to protect yourself from negative stimulation, or expose yourself

to less negative stimulation? (For example, stay away from colleagues who make you feel anxious, or try not to get sucked into conflicts between colleagues.)

o How can you ensure that the positive stimulation does not tip over and become negative? What can you do to regulate your stimulation and energy levels?

o Do you ever feel unstimulated or bored by your work? (Are you ever bored, depressed, find you have too much time on your hands?)

o What can you do to address the boredom? (For example, you could ask to go on a training course, volunteer to sit on a committee that's new to you, or speak to your manager about taking on more responsibility.)

Remember that everybody is different. Some people like a lot of stimulation and excitement, some like a little, and some like none at all. The purpose of this book is to help you get clarity on what does and doesn't work for you at work. Don't get caught in the trap of thinking about what other people experience, or what you think you should experience. Be perfectly honest with yourself when you think about this (and all other) tasks, and tell yourself the truth!

Resistance and aversion

There are sometimes some things about our work that make us want to either reduce our pace or come to a complete stop. This is what I call 'putting on the brakes'.

Imagine that you're hungry, and you're served a plate of food that looks and smells unappetising. Because you're hungry, you eat it, but it's tasteless. So it takes a long time, a lot of effort and some discomfort to clean your plate. That's what resistance feels like: you don't really want to do something, but you manage to get yourself through it, even if you may be kicking and screaming on the inside.

Now imagine that you're hungry, and the plate of food that's put in front of you is piled with all the things that make you sick when you eat them. You know you should eat it because you're hungry and need the fuel, but you just can't bring yourself to. That's what aversion feels like: that feeling that You. Just. Can. Not. (And it's a signal from yourself that maybe you just should not.)

Another way of thinking about it is that resistance is a slowing down, while aversion is a swerving away from an object. In terms of our behaviour, both are achieved by putting our foot on our figurative brakes. Those brakes – that physical feeling of revulsion and resistance we experience in response to an unwelcome thought or task – can range from soft (having a bowl of popcorn rather than cooking a meal), to moderate (avoiding an unpleasant task until it becomes urgent), to hard (flat-out refusing to do something/go somewhere/see someone).

We may use the brakes to keep ourselves safe, to avoid something unpleasant or to save us from boredom. The brakes are how we try to put a stop to doing, or thinking about doing, whatever it is that's making us feel bored or blah.

Most of us feel resistance and/or aversion (to varying degrees) in response to at least one aspect of our working world.

Asking the three questions covered in on page 80 (what am I feeling, why am I feeling this way, and what do I want to do about it?) will help you to clarify if you're feeling resistance or aversion.

If it's resistance that's causing you to apply your brakes, it's possible to figure out what you're resisting (boredom, being asked to do something that you don't feel capable of doing, or feeling at odds with a task or the person who has assigned the task) and take steps to address it so you feel less resistant, and more able and willing to roll up your sleeves and get on with it.

> Ask yourself: why am I resisting this? What is causing the tension between me and this task? It may be that you're tired or bored or don't understand it, or you're anxious that you won't do well enough at it, which may make you put off starting it.

AVERSION

Most of us have had the Sunday-night blues – that 'I haven't done my homework' feeling of misery and anxiety in anticipation of going in to the office again after a weekend of fun and relaxation. It's perfectly normal and very common, and for those of us who are lucky enough to enjoy our work, it generally passes on its own, and we've forgotten all about it when we wake up on a Monday morning, feeling motivated and excited about the week ahead.

But for some people, the anxiety about going into work is neither mild nor transient; they feel deep-seated aversion to it.

Long ago, I met someone who used to vomit copiously every Sunday night. Despite assuring herself and everyone around her that she loved her work, the thought of going back to work the next day literally made her sick to her stomach, week after month after year. More recently, I heard of a chap who was excellent at his job and really liked the work itself, but the environment and culture were so toxic that he would wake up and vomit before work. Every morning! For years!

These two rather extreme physical responses point to not just a dissatisfaction with work, but to a profound conflict about being there.

If you have an aversion – a visceral, no-way-I-can-ignore-this, slamming on the brakes feeling – to some or all aspects of your work, you really do need to do some serious thinking about where you are and if it's possible to make whatever is troubling you any better. That aversion is your body's way of telling you that what you're doing is not right for you – and quite possibly might not be right at all.

It's important to make sense of and learn from the aversion by interrogating why it's happening. Ask yourself:
o   What am I trying to avert or avoid by swerving away?
o   Why am I so averse to it?
o   Is it something I need to alert anybody else to?
o   Can I say 'no' to doing it?

When we believe our aversion to something (or someone), we can take steps to ensure our safety and wellbeing, and save ourselves from a lot of dis-ease and possibly even danger.

Procrastination, or putting something off, is an issue of resistance. It's an issue that many of my clients struggle with – but as soon as they understand that procrastination is a form of resistance, it becomes easy for them to do what needs to be done with self-compassion.

It's important to understand that we don't procrastinate because we don't want to be productive; rather we do so in an attempt to avoid the difficult feelings and emotions that come up when we're faced with certain tasks. We procrastinate when doing something – or thinking about doing something – is uncomfortable.

For some of us the discomfort we are trying to save ourselves from is simply boredom. For many people, the idea of doing something imperfectly, or admitting that they aren't completely sure about what they should be producing or how they should be producing it, is so anxiety-provoking that it feels easier in the moment to not do it at all.

Leaving a task to the last minute is the only way that many of us are able to deliver the goods; by pushing ourselves to the point of no-more-wiggle-room, we create a situation where the anxiety of not delivering at all outweighs the anxiety of not delivering perfectly. Unfortunately, although it may seem like we're being kind to ourselves by putting off a task, we're actually exacerbating the anxiety of not being able to do the task well enough by adding the angst of not doing the task at all.

Being a champion putter-offer, I was interested to learn that there are active and passive procrastinators. Active procrastinators have come to terms with the fact that, for them, less time makes for more action and so they factor this into their time and task planning. Passive procrastinators, on the other hand, keep kicking the can down the road until they run out of road and have no more reasons not to deliver the goods.

Both active and passive procrastinators delay doing certain tasks, but active procrastinators mindfully choose to start those tasks close to the delivery time and get on with other activities in the meantime, while passive procrastinators continue to beat themselves up for avoiding doing the task – all the way up to the usually last-minute point of completing it.

It's useful to understand your personal procrastination profile so that you can work with it, rather than against it. Ask yourself:

○ What do I avoid doing?

○ Why do I avoid doing it? Am I anxious I'll get it wrong? Am I anxious it won't be perfect? Am I unsure what needs to be done? Would I rather be doing something else? Is there something about doing it that feels wrong to me? Am I bored?

○ Am I avoiding it because of a resistance or aversion? (Am I slowing down or swerving?)

○ What do I want to do about it?

○ Can I ask for help?

As a procrastinator, I have learned that actively planning the most effective times to undertake and complete projects is an anxiety- and self-loathing-reducing game-changer. Giving myself permission to schedule certain tasks in a few days' or weeks' time is often the kindest and most constructive thing I can do for myself. Allowing myself some time and thinking space helps me to acknowledge why I'm resisting getting started (often anxiety that it won't be good enough or boredom), and what I can do to help myself get going.

My clients usually find that, at work (and at home), they generally have either too many tasks to do in the time they have available, or they have too much time and not enough tasks. Both of these situations can contribute to procrastination, either because of anxiety and feeling overwhelmed when there's too much to do, or because of complacency when there's too much time.

My late father always used to observe that I was the personification of Parkinson's law, which says that the work expands to fill the time allowed – I could drag something out to take up as much time as there was available. This meant that I spent much longer doing (or avoiding doing) tasks than was needed. I've since learned that reducing the time I have available to do a task makes me much more likely to do it – not just more quickly, but at all.

It sounds paradoxical, but the more we have to do, the more we get done, and the less time we have, the more productive we become in that time. If we limit our productive time, we will be more productive. And then we can spend the time outside of that doing other things – tasks that may feel gentler, less intensive and more rewarding.

Try this five-step plan to deal with procrastination:

1. *Revisit* the brief to make sure you know exactly what needs to be done. Often, we feel delivery anxiety when we're not entirely clear on what's expected of us. Going back to the beginning and asking for specific outcomes and expectations helps us to manage anxiety by creating more certainty around the task.

2. *Renegotiate the terms* of delivery to include a draft or two so that you can get some feedback along the way. Even with a clear set of outcomes, we're often prone to worry that we're not going to deliver a perfect product. I get around this by negotiating the submission of a first draft (even if it's the first draft of a proposed agenda) for feedback, so that I can ensure that I'm on the right track early on in the task proceedings. It's as simple as saying, 'Do you mind if I do a quick first pass at this and bring it to you for your input, so I know I'm on the right track with what you want and need from me?'

3. *Reframe any resistance* to the task so that it feels less scary and overwhelming. Our minds can be fertile gardens of thoughts and fears about what could possibly go wrong. When I catch myself raising the fear and anxiety stakes, I pull out some of the weeds by reframing my thoughts. 'What if they hate it?' becomes 'I wonder what feedback I will get and what changes I may need to make'; 'I can't do this' becomes 'I can do my best and that is usually more than good enough'; and 'This is so boring' becomes 'The sooner I finish this, the sooner I can do something more interesting'.

4. *Reduce the time* allocated. Shrinking the time allowed means less dithering and more delivering. Where procrastination is concerned, less is definitely more!

5. *Reward yourself* when the task is completed. I believe that recognising and acknowledging progress and completion are very important – and often overlooked – parts of any task. So, when you've got past all your fears, anxieties and obstacles, and have dotted the i's and crossed the t's, give yourself the recognition and reward you deserve for a job well done.

As with everything, being mindful and making a conscious choice about how you want to be at work and in the world will help you to understand and manage your procrastination – and make work work better for you.

LISTEN TO YOUR BODY

Resistance and aversion are both very physically felt invitations to examine what needs to change in your working day to make it feel more meaningful and rewarding.

We've already recognised how we can become more and more habituated to our physical space the longer we're in it, but it isn't just our external environment that we stop paying attention to over time. Our internal environment also gets overlooked, especially when we're stressed or busy or in survival mode. In fact, the more hassled or harried we are, the more we detach from our feelings. Just as we become inured to flickering lights or beeping inverters in our workspace, we learn to block out the discomfort we're experiencing inside ourselves.

But the signals our bodies are sending us are extremely important sources of information about what is and isn't working for us, at work and elsewhere. This is why I encourage my clients to check in with themselves as often as possible by becoming still and quiet and asking themselves the three magic questions: What am I feeling? Why am I feeling this way? What do I want to do about it?

The process doesn't only help us to identify that we have a headache because we need to drink more water, or that we're tired from staying up too late, it also helps us to stop ignoring the way we're feeling about our work and various aspects of it.

Using the Sunday-night blues I used to experience in my horrible job as an example, my answer to 'What am I feeling?' would have been 'Miserable at the idea of going back to work tomorrow'; to 'Why am I feeling this way?' would have been 'I hate the space, the work is boring, and I would rather not have anything to do with my helicopter boss'; and to 'What do I want to do about it?' would have been 'Stay at home and pretend I'm sick' (and I did that quite a lot). Now that I'm older and wiser, I realise that what I should have done was to remove or improve what I could, ask for more challenging work, or study something part time that I could work on during office hours when I had finished my 'job work'.

As was the case with my horrible job, some of your problems may make you bored and others may make you want to run screaming for the fire-escape multiple times a day. With some creative thinking, you can figure out where any work-related discomfort originates from, and how you can remove or improve many of the issues.

We all apply the brakes to countless things – many of the issues on your list of what doesn't work for you that we drew up on page 12 were probably inspired by them. Resistance and aversion, while unpleasant and certainly not very productive, are also transient. They're generally task- or place-related, and pass when the task is complete or the place is vacated; they're the kinds of things to which we can apply the 'remove or improve' principle.

However, if you feel an ongoing, generalised sense of exhaustion, being overwhelmed, resistance and aversion, you may be dealing with a more systemic problem. It may be that you have the dreaded burnout.

If there's no respite from the feelings of exhaustion, feeling overwhelmed, irritability or lack of motivation – even when you're doing things that should or used to make you happy and inspired – there's a good chance you have burnout. If you feel just as irritable, sad, unmotivated, withdrawn, sick, confused and questioning when you are away from work (on the weekends, away on holiday, playing with your kids, spending time with friends) as when you are at work, you need to manage your burnout so that you can rebuild your resilience and address your boredom and aversion.

Refer to pages 79 – 85 for more about dealing with burnout.

Showcasing your strengths

Some years ago, Marcus Buckingham, author of the 2001 bestseller *Now, Discover Your Strengths* and 2009's *Find Your Strongest Life*, interviewed a bunch of managers in top-performing companies to help him understand what they were doing to get the results they were achieving. What he discovered was that the managers of all the best teams got the most from their staff by encouraging them to focus on their strengths rather than on their weaknesses.

It's a little counter-intuitive because since childhood most of us have been told to try harder in areas that we 'could do better' in. From school reports to performance reviews at work, our 'development areas' are identified and presented to us. We're commended for being good at one or two things, but we're strongly encouraged to work harder at the things we're not that good at.

There are a couple of problems that unfold from this. First, if we're prone to judging ourselves without mercy and constantly seek approval and affirmation, then the feedback about what we're good at generally gets lost in the panic and anxiety that's generated by being told where and how we're not good enough. Second, there's a very real danger of de-emphasising and diluting what we are excelling at.

Attending to our development areas is all good and well, as long as the time and effort we spend developing what we're not so competent at does not detract from our ability to get even better at what we already do well.

When our strengths aren't encouraged or allowed to grow, there's a danger that they may wither. This is why, whenever I do a Wheel of Life (see page 161) or Wheel of Work (see page 6) exercise with my clients, I encourage them to identify what they can *keep doing* to maintain their higher levels of satisfaction while *starting to do* some things to increase their lower satisfaction areas.

As Buckingham points out, we all have different (and unique) strengths and weaknesses. One person's weakness is another person's strength, and vice versa. If we were all allowed – encouraged, even – to put most of our attention and energy into the things that we're good at, then a natural balance would prevail.

When we waste our efforts trying to get better at something that someone else already does well, we not only prevent ourselves from excelling at our strengths, we are also getting in the way of other people excelling at theirs. Similarly, when we allow ourselves to get better at what we're already good at, the things that we're 'weak' at may be compensated for by someone for whom they are strengths.

The unique strengths, or 'super-powers', as they are often referred to, that we all possess are a combination of all of our life's experience and learnings, as well as our innate skills – those things that we were born with an ability to do well. For example, my super-power is reading: not only books, but also moods, people, atmosphere, undercurrents, feelings, emotions, themes, trends – you name it, I can read it, mostly without even trying.

Buhle (see page 63) was a champion at juggling many tasks and people, while easily finding workable solutions to the problems she was quickly able to analyse and understand. Her childhood had prepared her to manage many little projects simultaneously, anticipate and meet the needs of the people around her, and do her own work very well in whatever little time she had available. She was also born clever, creative and curious, which all helped her to be a champion problem solver – which is her super-power.

Ideally, your work should allow you to make the most of your strengths, or at the very least keep them alive and well, in a sustaining and sustainable way. However, because our super-powers are so powerful, it's easy to apply them without being aware that we're doing so. Sometimes our super-powers lead us to do things that not only exhaust us, but which demand that we keep wearing that super-power cape, like Buhle, who constantly found herself solving other people's problems, to the detriment of her own time and energies.

The trick is in learning how to showcase our strengths without disempowering ourselves.

If you're not sure what your super-power is, or if you are not making the most of it, the following exercise should you to clarify how best you can showcase it at work:
o   Write a list of all of the very many things you're good at. Hint: we're usually good at what we enjoy, and enjoy doing what we're good at.
o   Bearing all your skills in mind, what is/are your unique strengths – your super-power/s?
o   How are you showcasing your super-power? Are you able to grow it and make the most of it?
o   If your super-power isn't getting the attention it deserves, how can you remedy that?
o   Are you misusing your super-power in a way that's working against you?
o   At work or at home, how can you pay attention to your strengths and make them even stronger?

When we allow ourselves to pay attention to what we're good at, we get even better at those things. When we allow ourselves to learn more, grow more and experience more, we enhance our strengths.

Can you think of two or three 'tiny' habits that will help you to improve your level of satisfaction in this area and allow your Wheel of Work to give you a smoother ride?

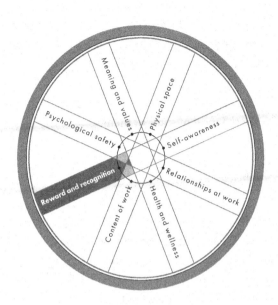

Reward and recognition

Psychologist and 'father of lateral thinking' Edward de Bono said that we all 'need to feel noticed and appreciated'. This is as true for adults looking for affection and affirmation from romantic partners as it is for children craving the attention of their parents – and wanting recognition for our efforts at work is no different.

We all want our endeavours to be seen, not because we're self-centred but because we put a lot of time and energy – and often our heart and soul – into our work, and it's important to get feedback on how we're doing. If we don't get that feedback, it's hard to keep putting in the same levels of energy and enthusiasm.

Recognition plays an essential role in motivating staff and contributing to job satisfaction. Of course, financial rewards in the form of salary and benefits such as medical aid and retirement investments are important, but, interestingly, one of the most significant factors in employee retention is recognition. A study conducted by American analytics and advisory company Gallup in 2017 found that, even though 89 percent of employers believed that staff left their companies for a better salary, most staff members who resigned said that a lack of recognition was a major contributor to their decision to look for greener – and more appreciative – pastures.

Recognition comes in many forms, even though we may not always recognise or make the most of some of them.

Feedback

Feedback is a critical element of recognition – but 'feedback' is such a loaded word. Feedback gets a bad rap because it's associated with having our weaknesses or flaws pointed out to us in a stress-laden meeting with the boss. For many people, it's loaded with associations of being hauled over the coals for doing something badly or not at all.

Receiving feedback can be scary, especially if we're prone to judging ourselves without mercy and seeking approval and affirmation, because those of us who do these things generally hear more of the 'could do better' messages than the 'did this well' ones. Receiving feedback is much scarier if it only happens once a year, like an end of year school report that determines if we will promoted to a higher class or need to repeat the one we have just completed.

In order to grow and develop consistently and incrementally, we need to have constant and consistent feedback and advice on what we could be doing differently or better. Unfortunately, annual performance-review processes are too often the only time any feedback is provided to staff members, and there's often not sufficient time to give thorough and meaningful feedback to help the recipient to grow into their role.

We don't only grow once a year; development is a continual and iterative process. By making feedback part of our culture, we help ourselves and others to learn, and to learn to think.

'I know she's very busy and stressed, but I wish my manager was better at giving me feedback on my work,' Ruth told me. 'I send in my reports, and not only do I

not get any sense of whether or not she's happy with my work, she doesn't even acknowledge the late nights and long hours that it took to get it done. All she does is give me more work to do as soon as I hand over what I was busy with. The only times she interacts with me is when she gives me another project or asks me when the various projects I'm already busy with will be delivered.'

Ruth continued, 'At university I had my marks to gauge how I was doing on each assignment I submitted. Now I get nothing – no indication of if I've passed or failed in the work assigned to me, or how well or badly I'm doing. Just radio silence and more work. I'm terrified that one day my manager is going to call me in and tell me I'm fired for underperforming – without me even knowing that I was!'

I find this complaint exasperating – not because the person making it is tiresome, but because the environment they work in is so maddeningly cruel and clueless. It's so simple and so impactful to take a few minutes to call a person in or drop them an email to thank them for a job well done – or even to ask them to do something differently.

Sadly, Ruth's frustration at being left out in the development wilderness is very common, certainly among many of the clients I work with. I think that it's no coincidence that many of my clients who are experiencing burnout complain about not getting the recognition they need and deserve at work. These clients are usually young professionals starting out in the world of consulting and project management. They're very clever and accomplished in their studies, and keen to make their mark in the real world, but they're also in need of some mentoring and guidance as to how to do so – academic aptitude and brilliance are wonderful, but don't always translate directly into the world of work.

For Ruth and all her peers who are high achieving (and usually more than a little anxious), being thrown into the deep end by managers who clearly trust them to do a good job, but who don't provide any much-needed emotional support and practical guidance, is stressful and scary. The Ruths of the world – and there are so very many of them – aren't looking for constant and unconditional positive comments; they genuinely want advice on how they can do better and succeed at the jobs they've chosen.

Feedback is vitally important if we are to understand what we can and should be doing to improve our performance, or even what we may be doing wrong. And not receiving any can be as stressful and anxiety-provoking as being given too much of it.

If you are in the same boat as Ruth, here are some of the actions she found helpful:

o   Ask for feedback. Be brave and explain how important it is for you to do well in your work, and how crucial feedback is for you to achieve that.

o   If your direct manager or boss isn't willing or able to give you feedback, find a substitute — identify an empathic person who is more experienced than you and ask if they would be willing to go through your work and give you their views on how you're doing.

o   Approach your HR office or someone else you deem to be appropriate and request that you be assigned a mentor.

As scary as it is to ask for this sort of help, if you (from your Adult ego state) are able to explain that you're seeking the support to do better and advance in the company, you'll be showing that you're aiming to get even stronger, rather than showing weakness.

GIVING FEEDBACK

If you're a manager who has a Ruth on your team, make the time and space to provide them with the guidance and input they're so hungry for and that they deserve. Have regular debriefing sessions with your team so you can collectively identify what went well and what didn't work out with the projects you are working on. Make individual and team development possible by ensuring that learning from mistakes, asking questions and being enquiring are part of your day-to-day operations.

When giving feedback, be compassionate and constructive, and offer solutions and practical ideas for what could or should be done differently or better – and how to go about it. Affirm your team members when they've made a useful point in a meeting or submitted a good report. Coach them when you think they could have done something in another way. And even though you may feel like shouting if they mess up, try to be a challenger rather than a bully (as we discussed on pages 68 and 69) by asking them to tell you what was going on for them when they made the point/took the decision/wrote the recommendation that was sub-optimal.

(discussed on pages 68 and 69)

RECEIVING FEEDBACK

Being on the receiving end of feedback isn't always easy. As much as we crave guidance and want to be told how we're doing, occasionally – especially if we're very hard on ourselves – feedback can be very difficult to hear and even harder to accept. It can be a challenge to get over our shame at not being perfect at everything all the time, to give ourselves permission to be human, and to learn and grow appropriately.

If you've received an evaluation that wasn't all glowing gold stars and full marks, it's useful to ask yourself (preferably with the support of a mentor or coach, but writing about it will also help) the following questions:

o   What do I agree with?

o   What makes me feel uncomfortable? Why?

o   What do I want to do with/about the feedback?

o   What do I want to pay attention to in order to improve where I need to and get different feedback in future?

o   What could I do differently?

As with many things in life, take what you can and make the most of every feedback experience. Try not to take things personally but see them objectively and from your Adult ego state, so that you can work with the feedback rather than against it.

Money

The research that shows that recognition is as important as, if not more so, than reward in retaining staff is borne out in my own coaching practice. When I ask clients to fill out the Wheel of Work, I'm often inspired by how many of them are willing to do work they love in environments that support them even though the financial compensation isn't what they could be earning elsewhere. Especially for people who are starting out in their careers and don't have large family financial commitments, the opportunities afforded by experience and exposure – and affirmation – in the workplace can be far more valuable than the money that arrives in their bank accounts every month.

This is not true for everyone, and certainly not for every phase of life; the corollary of this is how far generous salaries and benefits go in counteracting dissatisfaction with the actual work. (I'm not so surprised by how many of the people who stay in jobs they hate for the money they earn are on the road to, or have arrived at, destination burnout.)

Whether you love your job more than your salary, or your salary more than your job, there's no doubt that money is important, and reward in the form of salary and benefits is a major role-player in our work satisfaction.

Unfortunately, not many of us are raised to be comfortable talking about either money or our own worth. We hope that others will not only notice and appreciate us, but also reward us, without our having to ask them to. So we work hard and do our jobs well, and wait for the annual increase that indicates how much we are valued.

There's a difference between an annual increment that everyone gets as part of the budget cycle, and an increase in salary – possibly tied to a promotion – that's reflective of an appreciation of your growth and development in your role.

In organisations with big teams and many staff members, it isn't always easy to identify the people who deserve to be rewarded for the effort they put in. There are so many moving parts that it's hard to identify the most vital ones – unless they draw attention to themselves. And that's really what asking for a salary increase is all about: drawing attention to the valuable contributions you make so that you can be recognised and rewarded for them.

Even though it can feel deeply uncomfortable and a little bit risky to put ourselves in the spotlight and to ask for more (What if they think I'm greedy? What if they decide I'm under-performing even though I think I'm over-delivering? What if they think I'm arrogant and full of myself?), asking for a raise is a pretty normal practice. If you know and can show that you've been adding value in excess of your salary cheque, you can rest assured that asking for a raise is a perfectly acceptable thing to do.

Think of yourself as an artist. When a painter starts out, their works sell for a certain amount. As they gain more experience and their abilities grow and develop, the paintings they produce command higher prices in recognition of their increased proficiency and skill. People who appreciate art know this, which is why collectors are always on the lookout for new talent whose work they can buy up at affordable prices before they get too expensive. Your work is similar: you may not be creating works of art, but as you hone your skills and gain important experience, you and whatever you produce become more valuable and valued.

If you haven't received a merit raise (not a budget increment) in a year or more, perhaps it's time to prepare a motivation. In it, include:

- An outline of the work you've done in the last 12 months.
- A description of how you've added value to the projects you've worked on, the team you're a part of, and/or the company as whole.
- A list of all your responsibilities at work, including the number of people and projects you may be responsible for managing, as well as the non-paid work you do, such as volunteering or sitting on additional committees.
- Information about learning and development programmes you've participated in or completed.
- How getting an increase or promotion will empower you to do even better for the organisation.

Be conscious of choosing a good time to make your pitch; asking for a meeting to request a raise during a stressful deadline-driven time of year may not be the best idea.

Once you have gathered all this information together, written up a motivation and set up the meeting at an amenable time, you can start to think about how best to communicate your request. Imagine what your best Adult self would say – how would they calmly and confidently make their pitch? It may look something like this:

> 'Thank you for taking the time to meet with me today. I wanted to acknowledge how much I enjoy working here and how much I appreciate the opportunities I've been given to grow. I really value the experience I'm developing and hope that my work reflects not only this but also the value I add to the company. I'd like to discuss the possibility of a salary increase/promotion to the next level, and here's why I think I'm justified in this request.'

It's scary to put yourself out there by asking for a raise but remember your development and the concurrent increase in the value of what you produce. If you prepare your motivation, and present it mindfully and with confidence, you will not be judged for asking.

You may not get the results you want immediately, but taking this step will put you on the radar for future growth opportunities as well as greater rewards. It's a risk well worth taking.

Recognising recognition

Receiving praise and getting a raise are the two most obvious forms of recognition by our bosses. Obviously, money is a very important motivator, especially in these days of financial hardship and struggle. But it's important to recognise that there are many other ways that companies and managers can show recognition and appreciation of staff members – and, as we know, many of these approaches are far more valuable than a salary increase of a couple of percentage points once a year.

Because we generally think of recognition as coming in the form of a reward (a raise, a bonus, a spa voucher), we're not always able to appreciate the many other ways we're being recognised, and there are many. They include:

- Being thanked for a job well done.
- Being asked to mentor a new member of staff.
- Being asked to sit on a committee or a team.
- Being given time off after a busy period at work.
- Being asked to represent the company at a conference or an event.
- Being asked for our advice and opinions.
- Being encouraged to attend training and development programmes.
- When our personal situation is acknowledged and we're allowed to work from home or flexibly for a period.

One day, Ruth told me that her manager was sending her to an industry event where she would be expected to accompany and assist one of their major clients to prepare a presentation on their turnaround strategy (the strategy that Ruth had submitted so many reports on). She would need to catch a plane with the client, stay in the same hotel as him, and accompany him to dinner, as well as providing backup for the big presentation by brainstorming possible questions and answers the client may face.

She was excited and nervous in equal measure. What if she gave bad advice, did a bad job, let the client down...?

These were all the understandable fears that she brought to her coaching session. Before we got into dissecting and dispelling these fears, I asked Ruth if she thought that this honour (and it was a huge honour) was not just a vote of confidence in her by her manager, but also her manager's way of recognising and rewarding Ruth for her contribution to the project.

She thought about it for a few seconds before she nodded and smiled. It may not have been a substitute for the ongoing feedback and mentoring that she so wanted and needed, but this validation of her and her abilities was another form of recognition that took Ruth to a new level of assurance in herself and her competence.

It can be hard for us to notice and appreciate ourselves – and to notice and appreciate the recognition we're being given. We're often very quick to look for where and how we're not good enough. Like Ruth – so anxious about not being given obvious feedback – we look for evidence that proves how not-good-enough we are and overlook the evidence of our more-than-good-enoughness.

It's useful and enlightening to take some time to think about how you are recognised and what you are recognised for at work. Ask yourself:

- What do you think you do well at work? What are you most pleased with yourself for accomplishing at the end of the day/week/month/year?
- What about you and the work you do would you like to be noticed and appreciated by your colleagues and superiors? How can you draw attention to the work that you feel proud of?
- In what way are you recognised at work?
- Would you like to get different recognition? If so, how can you go about communicating that?
- How well do you notice and appreciate others in the workspace? Often the best way to get what we want to receive is to give it to others.

When we're able to recognise that appreciation and applause come in many guises, it can help us to feel less overlooked, and more noticed and appreciated.

DO YOU RECOGNISE AND REWARD YOURSELF?

It's also important that we're able to recognise our own achievements and reward ourselves for them, rather than only valuing what's seen and appreciated by others. Those of us who err on the side of self-judgement can find it hard to acknowledge when we've done a job well, often shifting the self-imposed goalposts so that we never feel we're winning, no matter how hard we try or how much evidence of our success there is. We feel we need to do more, learn more, earn more, try harder, push ourselves faster… There's always further to go.

It's disheartening to feel we will never reach whatever far-flung and unattainable destination we set out to get to. This is why we coaches are so insistent that our clients celebrate the victories, both big and small, that they achieve along the way. It's much easier to keep going and reach our destination when we recognise and celebrate the milestones, than if we're running blind and relentlessly.

Ask yourself:

o   What past victories, big or small, have you overlooked?

o   How can you acknowledge and celebrate them now?

o   Are there any milestones you're approaching that you would like to recognise? How will you do that?

What are some of the best ways you can think of to notice and appreciate yourself when you've done something noteworthy? From an exotic holiday or a new pair of shoes to celebrate the conclusion of a big project, to a nice cup of coffee or a bunch of flowers to reward yourself for getting through a boring report or a tricky meeting, any way you choose to acknowledge yourself will add immensely to your happiness at work.

Although our salary package is the most obvious indicator of how worthy our employer perceives us to be, reward and recognition come in many other guises. When we're able to recognise all of the ways that we're being noticed and appreciated, our work works better for us.

Can you think of two or three 'tiny' habits that will help you to improve your level of satisfaction in this area and make your Wheel of Work able to give you smoother ride?

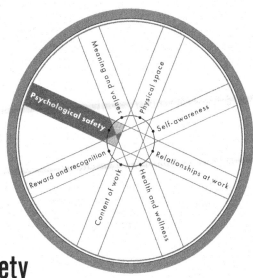

Psychological safety

'I know I have good ideas but I'm too scared to raise them.'

Yasmin was frustrated with herself and with her work. She had been in her position for a couple of years and was hoping to be promoted but had been disappointed a couple of times. When she worked up the courage to go and speak to her manager about why this kept happening, her manager told Yasmin it was because she was too quiet, and it was too easy to overlook her. The feedback was that Yasmin delivered work of an exceptionally high quality, but that she was never mentioned when the promotions team met because she was seen (when she was noticed at all) as a hard worker but not a leader or a visionary.

This is what prompted Yasmin to come for coaching and to lament the unfairness of her lot. And it really did seem unfair that someone as clever, creative, talented and bright as Yasmin clearly was, felt too unsafe to share her brilliance and ideas with her colleagues.

When I asked her what felt scary about speaking up, she explained that in her previous job she had mostly been ignored when she put up her hand in meetings.

On the odd occasion that she was given the floor, the team leader would roll his eyes, appear visibly unimpressed and check his cellphone the whole time Yasmin was talking, then shake his head and move on without acknowledging her inputs as soon as she had concluded her point. Obviously, Yasmin felt shamed and inadequate when this happened, so she eventually stopped putting her hand up and sat, silently seething with ideas and emotions, through every team meeting.

That would have been bad enough on its own, but when she discovered that the very same team leader had been promoted on the strength of presenting as his own one of the ideas she had put forward to dismissive eye-rolling, the humiliation was too much, and she handed in her resignation.

Obviously, that had been a very scarring experience for her and, understandably, Yasmin didn't feel safe enough to raise ideas or draw attention to herself in her new job. Unfortunately, though, her attempts to protect herself by not putting her head above the parapet ensured that she was never really seen properly nor was her brilliance recognised. She had taken her experience and expectation of an absence of psychological safety with her into her new workplace.

Even though, through coaching and on reflection, Yasmin was able to see that her current workplace was not as psychologically unsafe as the previous one was, her strategy of keeping her head down still felt like the safest way for her to be at work. Once she was able to recognise that her new working environment was not as fraught as the last one, she was able, bit by bit, to test the waters and start to share her ideas incrementally. The safer she felt, the more she opened up, and the more she was noticed and recognised by her peers and managers. I'm happy to report that she was offered a higher position in the very next round of promotions!

Psychological safety is a feeling that you can speak up, share ideas and be honest about who you are and what you think, without fear of being bullied, undermined, ridiculed or made to feel inadequate in any way. It's an expectation of belonging and acceptance by and for team members.

Amy Edmondson, the Harvard professor who coined the term, described it like this: 'Psychological safety means an absence of interpersonal fear. When psychological safety is present, people are able to speak up with work-relevant content.'

There is less defensiveness and threat in psychologically safe environments. *Psychologically Safe for Some, but Not All?*, a 2022 research study conducted by the Centre for Creative Leadership found that teams with high degrees of psychological safety reported higher levels of performance and lower levels of interpersonal conflict.

Workplaces that are psychologically safe allow the people within them to be fully, authentically themselves, and to offer suggestions, make and learn from mistakes, ask for feedback and be creative without fear of judgement or humiliation. When we feel psychologically safe, we feel confident to see and be seen, and to make contributions.

The opposite of psychological safety is psychological unsafety, which results in us moving into survival mode that sees us either freezing or fleeing in order to protect ourselves from humiliation or harm. Yasmin's survival strategy was to freeze – to go about her business as unobtrusively and invisibly as she could. Other people choose to flee, either by leaving the environment altogether, or by checking out and not engaging meaningfully with their work or anyone involved it.

Improving levels of psychological safety

When we have the kind of experience that Yasmin did, it has a deep and abiding impact on us. When we're in survival mode, we aren't able to be creative or excited, or put ourselves and our thoughts out there, because we're too busy protecting ourselves from possible shaming or danger. And we, as well as the organisation we're a part of, suffer. Diversity of thought and diversity of experience are critical elements of successful, learning teams and organisations, and the only way to ensure that the full benefit is gained is by creating psychologically safe spaces for people.

How psychologically safe do you feel at work? Ask yourself:

o   Do you feel safe to be yourself at work?

o   Do you feel secure that ideas you raise will be received honestly and honourably? Are you confident to make points, share ideas and challenge people who you don't agree with?

o   Are there people or situations that make you feel vulnerable or psychologically unsafe?

o   Are there any work practices, like remote or hybrid working, that contribute to making you feel (or be) overlooked, unrecognised and even forgotten about?

HOW TO IMPROVE YOUR LEVELS OF PSYCHOLOGICAL SAFETY

If you've identified that you feel less than safe in the workplace, here are some ideas to improve your levels of trust and confidence:

Test the waters slowly

Put forward a small idea, a tiny contribution, a tentative challenge, and see how it lands. It'll be a bit like walking into a lake that you can't see the bottom of – you can't tell if there are rocks, holes, crabs or other obstacles that may hurt you in some way – so you need to proceed slowly, carefully and cautiously, one small step at a time. This way, as soon as you become aware of an obstacle or some danger, it will be easy and manageable for you to step back to safety.

Find some allies

Be on the lookout for people who you feel you can trust to stand up for you and support you. Set up conversations to identify where and how you can help each other, defend each other and amplify each other. (Although do guard against the creation of an exclusionary clique.)

Do some problem-solving analysis

The most effective way to make any unsafe environment safe again is by getting to the root cause of the problem. You can start by identifying all the ways and all the times you've felt unsafe at work.

Make a long and comprehensive list. Then try to understand why that/those incidents felt unsafe for you. Ask yourself:

- o Did you feel overlooked or undermined or ridiculed or attacked?
- o Why do think that happened?
- o Is there a pattern of people who are undermined?
- o Is there a pattern of people who do the undermining?
- o Is there a pattern of places that this undermining takes place (e.g. in team meetings, in one-on-one interactions, in the tearoom)?

As soon as you notice a pattern of the kinds of people who tend to be undermined, you have a good start in finding your allies; approach (cautiously if need be) those who have a common experience of being undermined and ask for and offer support.

If you're able to identify the people who do the undermining, you can preemptively plan to have as little to do with them as possible and ask for extra support from allies when you have to engage with them.

Similarly, if you're able to pinpoint the kinds of forums or places where the danger is most prevalent, you and your allies will be able to improve the safety of yourselves and everyone else by going into those situations armed with strategies to protect yourselves, for example, your Adult role model (see page 38), the 'What makes you think that…?' questions (see page 141), and a commitment to amplify each other's ideas.

By doing any or all of these things, you'll immediately improve your own levels of psychological safety and create a ripple effect in the organisation. When you and the team you are a part of start to experience and demonstrate the value of feeling secure enough to be vulnerable, take risks and thus reap the creative rewards, the teams around you will almost certainly start to follow your lead.

Psychological safety does not create itself. It requires concerted and ongoing efforts from leadership in organisations.

'How do I get my team members to open up and be honest about what they're thinking, what they can and can't manage, and what they need help with?'

This was a straightforward question from Zara, but I hear variations of it often from clients who are frustrated with the lack of openness and participation from their team members. Through brainstorming ideas in her coaching sessions, Zara managed to create a safe space for her team members by modelling vulnerability and compassion. She instituted two items that topped every team meeting agenda: 'personal check-ins' and 'lessons learned'.

Zara opened each meeting with the 'three questions' exercise – by asking and answering the questions 'What am I feeling?', 'Why am I feeling this way?' and 'What do I want to do about it?' out loud [see page 80].

She then asked every team member to check in by sharing the insights that were generated by answering the three questions. The check-ins ranged from 'I'm feeling anxious because I've never had to do this kind of thing before but I'm going to give it a chance and see how it works out' to 'I have a headache because I had too much to drink last night at a friend's birthday party so I'm going to have a quiet and not very interactive day today' to 'I'm resentful that the suggestions I made last week were overlooked and I'd like a meeting to discuss why this happened and how I can refine the ideas to make them workable'.

Because Zara went first, those who followed felt they had been given permission to be honest, and within a very short time people were feeling brave enough to open up, be honest about their feelings and even ask for help where needed.

For the 'lessons learned' conversation, Zara led the vulnerability way again, by sharing an example of a mistake or a misjudgement she'd made in the previous week, presenting the lessons she'd learned from the experience, and asking her team members for their ideas about how she could have done things differently or better. This exercise served two purposes: it helped those present to make friends with the fact that we all mistakes, and it encouraged learning by the individuals and the team so that those mistakes were neither a waste of effort nor repeated.

The check-ins became one of the most important and highly valued aspects of team meetings, followed in appreciation by the 'lessons learned' conversation. By encouraging her team to be honest about their feelings and their experiences – both personal and professional – Zara was able, in a very short time, to create a team that felt psychologically safe, and consequently performed better and better.

Because we take our wounds to work with us, people who are in survival mode, or who have some of the characteristics of 'adult children', particularly those who guess what normal is, who judge themselves without mercy, who seek approval and affirmation, and who lie when it's just as easy to tell the truth (all covered in other chapters) struggle to feel psychologically safe at the best of times.

Even the kindest and most compassionate leader may struggle to get every member of their team to feel safe and secure. I believe it's always a good starting point to get some idea of the individuals in the team – where they each come from, what some of their struggles have been, and what some of their current challenges are. When we're able to see the people who make up our team as separate entities, each with their own anxieties and drivers, then we can work towards making a space that feels safe for everyone.

So many of my clients are just like Yasmin or Zara: eager and equipped to contribute to their team but not trusting enough to allow themselves to do so, or wanting to get the best out of their staff members but unsure how to go about opening a chink in their armour.

It doesn't matter if the lack of trust is historical or current; the crafting of organisational cultures committed to emotionally safe and secure working spaces is imperative if we are to reap the full rewards that come with all team members feeling safe enough to contribute their ideas. Creating and ensuring psychological safety is critical if we are to ensure the longevity and sustainability of teams and organisations.

Organisational culture and climate

The culture and climate of an organisation have a profound impact on work satisfaction, productivity and wellness at work, despite the fact that – or perhaps because – they are often intangible and difficult to recognise or describe.

Organisational culture is the collection of beliefs, values and norms that shape the behaviour of people within an organisation; it defines how staff members conduct themselves, how they do their work, and how decisions are made and communicated.

In their 1982 book *Corporate Cultures: The Rites and Rituals of Corporate Life*, organisational consultants Terry Deal and Allan Kennedy famously defined it as 'the way we do things around here'. It's a wonderful explanation and is as ethereal and contextual as the organisational cultures of individual companies are.

When undergoing transformation processes, organisations almost always identify their culture as being the first and most important thing to change – with good reason. Countless studies have shown that all aspects of an organisation – from levels of psychological safety, recognition and reward, to timekeeping and after-work drinks – are affected and influenced by its culture. And research shows that three-quarters of jobseekers consider the culture of a company before even applying for a position, with almost 50 percent of people who are employed reporting that they would take a reduction in salary to work in a place with a better culture.

Organisational climate, on the other hand, is the shared or common perception of employees about a company's policies, processes and practices, both formal and informal. The climate of a geographic area determines how people living there experience their environment; it can be calm, stormy, hot, cold, temperate, treacherous, filled with inhospitable pests... Organisational climates are the same: they are the lived and felt experience of the people who inhabit the space. What suits some people may feel too harsh or too dull for others.

The climate of an organisation relates to the atmosphere or feeling that people have at work, and is as important as culture in attracting and retaining talent.

The distinction between culture and climate is very useful in understanding the complexities of a stated or overt culture versus the lived climatic experience of the individuals who make up the society. One of the most fascinating things about organisations is the frequent gap between the overt, stated culture, and the covert, unacknowledged culture that is often much more prevalent and a powerful determinant of the climate.

One of the many jobs I've had was in an organisation that had a stated culture of inclusiveness, consultation, equality, transparency, non-sexism, non-racialism and all the other things that we should all be striving for. It was an amazing place to work, and I will always treasure my time and experience there. But it is only now that I'm much older, quite a bit wiser and a little less idealistic and starry-eyed that I can see that the climate was substantially different and more pervasive than the stated culture. There were a whole lot of informal practices that were at odds with the mission, vision and values that we were all so proud of.

Many of the elements of an inhospitable and, for some, a psychologically unsafe organisational climate could be found there: sexual innuendo, inappropriate remarks and behaviour, outright harassment, thinly veiled racism, cliques, favouritism, and race and gender bias. Although no laws were ever broken and the experience of working there was for the most part extremely meaningful, rewarding and enjoyable for most of the staff, there's no doubt in my more mature and more informed mind that there was a lot wrong with how things operated. For people on the receiving end of the subterranean culture (basically, everyone who wasn't a white man), their experience of the workplace – the climate – was at serious odds with the culture.

As with so much in life, it's easy to see the issues in hindsight, but they were not nearly as obvious when I was in the environment, partly because I was young and naïve, and partly because they were hiding in plain sight.

However, there's now much more awareness about the impact that culture *and* climate have on job satisfaction and staff retention. There's a great deal of attention being paid to diversity, equity and inclusion, and as workplaces become more diverse and inclusive, we're reaping the rewards of a wider range of experiences and approaches. But we're also faced with an ever-increasing realisation that 'how we do things around here' isn't always as comfortable or acceptable for everyone in the workplace.

Thanks to the #metoo and other movements and campaigns, much-needed attention is being placed on making working environments as comfortable, hospitable, safe and healthy for all that work there as possible. Still, in many organisations there's a long road to travel before we get to this destination.

We need to open up and encourage conversations about our histories and our backgrounds, our expectations and our experiences, so that we can develop a more inclusive and compassionate way of doing things. We need to open communication channels so that everyone feels more psychologically safe and brave enough to make contributions and participate fully in their working life.

The heavy loads that women bear at work

Research shows that the less attention being paid to diversity and inclusion, the more psychologically unsafe staff members feel, unless – again – those staff members are straight white men. It's unfortunate and not at all surprising that many of the people who feel least psychologically safe in the workplace are women.

The vast majority of the clients who come to me for burnout-recovery coaching are women. Some may argue (and I may agree) that this is because women are more comfortable with showing vulnerability and seeking help. And it's also true – studies prove it – that women are more likely to experience burnout than men are. I'm sure there are many reasons for this, chief among them the fact that women bear some responsibilities and burdens that men do not – burdens that make us very susceptible to exhaustion and burnout.

Women juggle a whole lot of roles and responsibilities: we're mothers, daughters, sisters, wives, friends, carers. We work both in and outside of the home. We play active roles in our communities. Of course, men also have multiple responsibilities, but it seems to me that my female clients are expected – by themselves just as much as by others – to play more roles than my male clients are.

The constant juggling of expectations, roles and responsibilities is very, very tiring.

Women are also very vulnerable. We're constantly on our guard, looking over our shoulders to check that we're safe, and experiencing a surge of adrenaline when we fear that we may not be. We're vulnerable to emotional and physical abuse and attack. We're vulnerable to exploitation.

SEXISM AND HARASSMENT

During the course of writing this book, I asked a number of groups of women to tell me about their biggest challenges as women at work. Without exception, the first things they mentioned were harassment and sexism.

At work, and on the way to and from work, women are exposed to uninvited and unwanted physical contact from men who seem to regard it as their birthright to fondle and touch any woman who crosses their path. The harassment also takes the form of leering and making sexual remarks to or about women and their appearance: the shape of their bodies, the clothes they wear, the way they walk… Not a lot of psychological safety for many women, then.

Sexism, or gender bias, is often a little more subtle and difficult to call out, but is perhaps even more prevalent in our patriarchal society. Being a woman in a man's world, even though it isn't nearly as exclusionary or 'manly' as it once was, is a lot to bear.

The sexism that is so top of mind for all the women who responded to my questions means that we must fight to prove ourselves, to be heard, to be taken seriously. We and our knowledge and ideas are often overlooked, negated, patronised or mansplained to. Keeping our tempers while fighting to be heard is very, very tiring.

When you look for it, you can see gender bias in the workplace all over. It's in the way women are talked over, how their ideas are scorned – often to resurface as the brainwave of a male colleague who's happy to take all the credit the idea now receives – or belittled. It's in the patronising chuckles and figurative head-patting with which the thoughts and inputs of women are so often dismissed. It's in the way women are left off the invitation list for important meetings or golf games, or overlooked when teams are put together for projects.

It's also in the way women are expected to do the non-core things at work – arranging farewell parties, socials, birthday cards, taking minutes in meetings – because we're 'so good at that kind of thing'. The only reason we're so good at it is because we have had so much practice! Men would be just as competent and accomplished if they gave it a try.

Even on social media, women are trolled and undermined and put down. Scrolling through LinkedIn recently, I came upon a post by a prominent and popular executive coach who was no doubt trying to be amusing in one of his frequent daily postings. 'When your man tells you he's going to buy a Porsche, there are only two questions to ask him,' he wrote: 'What colour? And what do you want me to be wearing when you bring it home?'

There followed some surprised and unamused replies, including mine, all along the lines of 'What patriarchal nonsense is this?' I then got a LinkedIn notification that let me know that the executive coach had found my comment funny! I wasn't even remotely amused, and wrote as much in a reply to him. How did he respond? He wrote, 'I invite you to view this from the full depth of your Feminine radiance...'

Two immediate lightbulbs went off in my brain. First, this interaction was infuriating enough on social media, with someone I've never met in person. It's so much more poisonous when this kind of provocation takes place (and I assure you, it does) between colleagues in the physical workplace, where the not-so-subtle undermining, gaslighting and negating of women adds to an environment of toxicity and alienation for women and anyone who doesn't subscribe to this macho culture.

And, second, this is why it isn't getting any easier for women in the workplace. How can we expect change when sought-after and highly paid 'elite personal and executive coaches' post such obviously sexist attitudes in public forums – and then continue the chauvinism by gaslighting the women who call them out on it?

Organisations are paying vast sums of money to coaches and consultants who are appointed to guide the leadership to oversee improvement and advancement in the organisations they consult to. If these consultants are masking their prejudice in the workplace but putting it on display in other places, they're not only clearly ambivalent about the changes they're being paid to lead, they will also unknowingly encourage the perpetuation of inhospitable and psychologically unsafe climates by entrenching the prevailing culture. When the worldview of the change consultants is stuck in the dark ages, it must contaminate the guidance they're providing to their clients.

Dealing with a patriarchal culture

When the culture and climate of an organisation is entrenched and enduring, it can feel extremely hard to question or push against it, particularly if questioning the status quo is met with derision or scorn. I've heard too many women berate themselves for becoming shrill in the face of being patronised, spoken over, ignored or dismissed in a variety of other ways. 'Why couldn't I just stand my ground and keep calm?' they think. 'I wish I hadn't lost my temper; I turned into some sort of screaming banshee.'

Losing your cool is horrible at any time, but to do it in an environment that seizes on it as evidence of your being too emotional, or irrational, or – the worst – hysterical, is deeply distressing.

As tempting as it is to react emotionally to unfair treatment or unjust assumptions, a far more powerful and empowering way to respond is by questioning the behaviour or assumptions that are generating the emotions. But that questioning can't take just any form – it needs to be a question that is confronting without being confrontational, that holds up a mirror, that forces the person being questioned to think about their thoughts and actions, and to take responsibility for them.

That question is 'What makes you think that...?'
* What makes you think that you know more about this than I do?
* What makes you think that I'm better at arranging staff teas than you?
* What makes you think that it's okay to say something like that?
* What makes you think that's funny?

141

- What makes you think that you can put your hands on me?
- What makes you think that it's okay to speak to me like that?

Asking a 'What makes you think that…?' question literally makes the person think about the answer and, hopefully, identify their assumptions and bias. It's less strident and accusatory than a 'why' question – 'Why do you think that's funny?' sounds (and feels) more accusatory than 'What makes you think that's funny?'

When we ask the 'What makes you think that…?' question from our calm, rational Adult state (see page 38), we're encouraging the person we're interacting with to think about their assumptions and hopefully get some insight into them. It's an invitation to learn and do better, rather than a war of words – confronting rather than confrontational.

Solidarity at work

Everyone who has found themselves on the outskirts of the dominant organisational culture and community knows about the subtle – and sometimes not so subtle – slights: the micro-aggressions, the eye-rolling, the ignoring, the speaking over; the kinds of things that make the climate of an organisation inhospitable.

These are the kinds of things that we almost expect to happen in our society and the microcosm of it that places of work tend to be. It is not acceptable and we need to fight to understand and change it, but it is perhaps more understandable than the thing that upsets my women clients (and me) the most – which is the lack of understanding and support from many of their female managers.

SISTERS WHO ONLY DO IT FOR THEMSELVES

The lack of 'sisterhood' in the work context is deeply distressing. Women often see their female peers being undermined and overlooked, and they don't speak up about it – not in public, anyway. And this is true not only for women but for any marginalised grouping in the workplace.

What is happening? Why are we regressing? Where is the solidarity and the sisterhood? While it has gone AWOL, it seems that so has the advancement of women (and others) and our rights.

I don't know if this lack of sisterhood is a result of exhaustion and running out of runway to fight the good fight – still, after all these decades of more diversity in the workplace. Or perhaps we're so thinly stretched with our own work and life demands that we don't have the wherewithal to notice or do anything about the things we see. Or maybe it's some kind of post-feminist, we-need-to-move-on-and-let-every-person-fend-for-themselves, no matter how unfair the treatment, scenario. Whatever the reason, I think we need to take a long, hard look at ourselves and our communities (in and out of work) and see what we can do to address the problem.

'PULL HER DOWN SYNDROME'

Another recurring theme that emerged from the women I spoke to about the challenges they face at work was what one person referred to as the 'pull her down syndrome'.

This is something that I identified as being disappointingly widespread in research I participated in almost 20 years ago. That study examined the role and impact of women managers in the public service. The most common and distressing finding was that women managers were both less sympathetic towards and expected more from their female staff members. Women managers were more lenient with male staff, and male managers were more supportive of female staff.

It's a horrible reality to digest, but the truth is that it's also kind of understandable. The more I work with women who work in cut-throat environments, the more I understand the fight to get ahead. In hostile environments, we become hostile.

Horrible female bosses

Every working woman has experienced being talked over, contradicted, ignored and/or put down, despite being the best informed and most qualified person in the room. 'You don't understand', 'You've got it wrong' and 'That's not how it works' are just a few of the dismissive remarks so many women have heard.

Is it any wonder women become hard and shrill? It is almost impossible to maintain your composure in such circumstances. And it's equally hard to avoid getting into an 'if you can't beat them, join them' frame of mind by adopting an equally harsh, unsympathetic, and unkind *modus operandi*.

'I hate what I'm doing! I'm turning into the woman I vowed I would never be. When I was a young professional, I used to look at the female managers who were uncaring and often aggressive towards the junior women in the organisation, and promise myself I would be the opposite when I became a manager. But all my ambitions of being compassionate, understanding and supportive seem to have dissipated. And I hate myself for it. Yesterday I literally rolled my eyes and sighed when one of my most promising junior managers came to tell me she's pregnant. What a kind of a monster does that?'

As horrifying and appalling as this sort of response may seem, as Brenda's coach I was deeply concerned for her. She was clearly in the midst of a downward spiral of self-loathing and recrimination.

As we spoke about her career trajectory and experiences at work, Brenda realised that she had become so tired of being told that she was soft or indulgent, or that she was 'spoiling' the female staff who would never progress through the ranks if she was too accommodating and kind, that she shut down her empathy and compassion and went to the other extreme. In an attempt to rescue herself from the constant negative messages about how she wasn't going to get ahead by being nice, she unthinkingly and unintentionally turned herself into a bully, taking out her own frustrations and disappointments on the younger versions of herself, and thus perpetuating the cycle of mean female bosses.

Brenda took a couple of weeks of much-needed leave to get a complete break from the office environment and do a hard re-set on herself. When she recovered from her exhaustion, she was able to soften up and reconnect with her inherent empathy. She was better able to see what had been happening, and she made a commitment to herself to return to being the thoughtful and generous person she liked and respected.

To help her with this, she wrote in a journal every evening to help her sort through her emotions and worries, and make sense of the interactions she had experienced that day. Just half an hour of journalling at the end of the day helped her to slow down, reconnect with herself, and gain important insights into the climate of her team and the broader organisation. It helped her to anticipate where, when and with whom she may need to put on a virtual raincoat to protect herself from those storms of judgement and criticism she had been so beaten down by, and when and who in her team she needed to hold an umbrella over to protect them from the harsh elements.

Within a couple of weeks of consistent journalling, Brenda could see that the parts of herself that she liked, and that had a positive impact on the people she managed, were starting to re-emerge. She was kinder, more compassionate and a lot more patient with her staff, and they blossomed and stepped up under her guidance and support.

In her final coaching session, Brenda reflected that 'the time of women trying to be like men to survive the work environment is over. What's the point of having more women in the workplace if we just become like men?'

I couldn't have said it any better!

In order to survive and advance, many women managers feel that they have no option but to assume a mantle of harshness and opposition. Unfortunately, this attempt to become and behave like someone they are not means that many women ignore their own innate strengths and abilities – trading in their empathy and intuition for competition and judgement.

When women overlook their so-called 'soft skills' and focus on harsher ways of getting more out of their staff, everyone loses: the manager who's in combat with herself as well as everyone else, the team members she's mismanaging, and the organisation itself. Additionally, pushing ourselves to be something we are not is definitely not the right thing for us, and is a clear (or certain) path to burnout .

We need to change the environment by changing how we are in it – by being authentic and congruent. Instead of trying to fit in or measure up, let's embrace our own strengths, abilities and talents.

A few decades ago, I participated in the women's movement at university. We looked out for each other, called out men who were sexist and demeaning, and ensured we got the respect and consideration we demanded and were due. We were a sisterhood.

A few years ago, women friends and colleagues would come to me behind closed doors to pledge support when there'd been incidents of sexism, discrimination, negating, gaslighting, undermining or patronising, and congratulate me (privately) when I called men out on this. They were silent supporters.

More recently, when I was undermined, patronised and minimised by the male executive coach on LinkedIn, not one woman showed support either publicly or privately. There are so many soloists, keeping their heads down in hostile environments.

If you speak up for women when you witness them being undermined, negated, humiliated or harassed, you're a sister. If you sidle up to women and speak your support after you've witnessed them being undermined, negated, humiliated or harassed, you're a silent supporter. If you turn a blind eye to the undermining, negating, humiliating or harassing of women you see, and focus on staying in your own lane, you're a soloist.

We're all just trying to survive a society that's stacked against women. But if we want to move past surviving into thriving – actively enjoying and feeling appreciated and acknowledged – we need to consciously and openly support each other. We need to stick together, stand up against injustice and inequality, and champion each other as a means to championing ourselves. We need to bring back the commitment to sisterhood.

It is equally important to speak up, rather than silently support or stay in your lane when and if you see unjust or unfair treatment of anyone – not just women – who you witness being mistreated in the work environment.

Whether you are a man or a woman, what 'tiny' things or habits can you start to do that will ensure that you help to pick those around you up? Ask yourself:

o   How can you call out sexist, homophobic, racist, scary or creepy behaviour when you see it or experience it?

o   How can you acknowledge and appreciate the good ideas that are presented by women or anyone else being marginalised, and ensure that the credit goes where it is due if the idea is being passed off as someone else's?

o   How can you amplify your own voice when you are spoken over or down to, or when someone speaks, uninvited, for you?

o   How can you attune your own ears so that you are able to hear what is being said by everyone, even if they do not look or sound like you?

We all have a role to play in contributing to the creation of psychologically safe spaces at work – spaces that allow people to not only take professional risks, but also to feel comfortable to be honest about who and how they are.

Be an advocate, find an advocate
A (non-legal) advocate is a person who publicly supports a cause or a policy, who speaks up for what is right and against what is wrong. We can all benefit from being an advocate as well as having someone to advocate on our behalf.

Who can you approach to be an advocate for you at work? Is there a person – and they don't have to be in your immediate circle in the organisation – who you can ask to play the role of picking you up?

Who can you be an advocate for? It's never a good idea to presume or to offer unsolicited support – unless you know what your colleague needs and wants from you, ask the question, 'How can I best help you?'

Be the best version of yourself in the workplace
Being brutally honest with yourself, what are some of the ways you think or behave at work that are not the best version of yourself? Maybe you're less empathic and more critical than you would like to be; maybe you're less forceful and assertive than you would like to be; or maybe the environment has made you hostile or hesitant.

147

What steps can you take to ensure that you can return to the best version of yourself?

Moving out of survival mode and into success mode

In the days of our ancestors, the need to be in survival mode was intermittent. They'd see a danger, hide from it, run from it, or punch it on the nose, and then they'd be safe again for a while. The part of us that keeps us alive (what I call our 'survivor self') only had to show up every now and then.

As life and the world have evolved, however, so have the dangers, both physical and emotional.

Even if you work in a team with high levels of psychological safety, there are inevitably some periods at work that feel stressful and scary. There are competing demands and strict deadlines and difficult bosses and disappointing colleagues, and this can all feel a little overwhelming and sometimes even dangerous.

After years of economic meltdowns, climate disasters and various other threats to our safety and wellbeing, it can feel as though our survivor self has assumed the lead role rather than playing a bit-part in the theatre of our lives. Some of us have been in survival mode for so long we can't remember how to be in normal, common-or-garden, just plain *living* mode – let alone being able to access the part of us that drives accomplishment and success.

When we're in survival mode, we're scared, anxious and stressed. We operate from a place of profound mistrust. We become very reactive to events and interactions, and we have little to no faith in anything going right for any length of time. We're hypervigilant, constantly on the lookout for danger or disappointment. Everything looks and feels like a threat, especially in the workplace, which is often less than relaxing.

It's hard to be the best and most successful version of ourselves when we're stuck in survival mode, when every day is just about getting through and making it to going-home time. We can't be creative or collegial when we're in survival mode.

And we can't move out of survival mode and towards success mode if we're feeling insecure and uncertain.

Next time that fear-based, mistrustful, anxious part of you starts to tell you that your personal extinction in imminent, try this:

- ○ Take a few deep, cleansing, calming breaths.
- ○ Think of a recent time when you were able to respond constructively to a threat (no matter how big or small). Try to remember the threat and your response in as much detail as possible.
- ○ Now, think of another time you were able to constructively respond to a threat (again, no matter how big or small). Again, try to remember the threat and your response in as much detail as possible.
- ○ Keep remembering times you were able to keep yourself safe in the face of danger until you feel calm and strong.

The best way to move away from survival and towards success is to create our own internal psychologically safe spaces by reminding ourselves to be the able and empowered Adults we really are.

Can you think of two or three 'tiny' habits that will help you to improve your level of satisfaction in this area and make your Wheel of Work able to give you smoother ride?

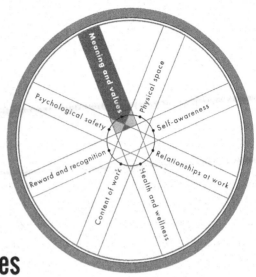

Meaning and values

In an ideal world, we would all be doing work that feels rewarding and worthwhile (meaning) while giving expression to the beliefs and principles we hold dear (our values).

The Great Resignation that took place in 2021 and 2022 has been attributed, in large part, to people seeking out jobs that felt like a better alignment with their personal values and meaning, and were therefore more personally rewarding. Unfortunately, in many countries there's widespread job scarcity, which makes work, for those who are lucky enough to have it, a means to an end rather than a meaningful expression of self.

In some cases, the money is the meaning.

Money versus meaning

In their 1959 book, *The Motivation to Work*, psychologists Frederik Herzberg, Bernard Mausner and Barbara Snyderman famously identified our motivations for working as being both 'extrinsic' and 'intrinsic'.

The extrinsic motivations are the tangible, measurable rewards that we get in exchange for doing our jobs – our salaries, the places where we do the work, and the conditions under which we work.

Intrinsic motivations are, as the name suggests, more internal to the individual and relate more directly to the character of each person. These include things like a sense of recognition, a feeling of fulfilment, and being able to showcase our creativity and strengths, and learn and grow and advance.

Extrinsic motivations have traditionally garnered most of the attention and emphasis given to understanding and (hopefully) improving working conditions. But over the past few decades, and no doubt due largely to the work of Herzberg, Mausner and Snyderman, more and more attention is being paid to the experience of the work itself, not just the environment in which it's conducted or the pay received for doing it. Now, there's much greater recognition of the importance and impact of both the culture and climate of the organisation, and the values and microclimate of the individual. Work is no longer just a means to a monetary end but is also an expression of what is important to us.

The meaning that we attach to our work is the manifestation of the deeper purpose of why we do what we do, and it's different for everyone. For some, the reason they work is to earn money to support their family, while for others making a contribution to science or the arts is what makes their work matter to them. For still others, the meaning their work provides for them is an opportunity for self-expression. When we look at meaning in this way, it's easy to see how important a role our values play in making work meaningful.

Whatever it looks like and feels like for you, being able to attach some meaning to your work is important not only for your job satisfaction but also for your contentment and general fulfilment. It's difficult to feel motivated and absorbed in your work when it doesn't feel meaningful and rewarding, and doing work that isn't absorbing or motivating is very alienating, and this can leave us feeling miserable and uninspired. And, of course, doing too much of the wrong thing – or spending too much time on work that does not feel personally important – is one of the biggest contributors to burnout.

In recent years, increasing emphasis has been placed on the importance of non-monetary reward and recognition in job satisfaction. As we have discussed, there are many aspects of work and the work environment that contribute to the experience and enjoyment of work. At its best, work is an expression of who we are, and provides opportunities for us to grow and learn and, most importantly, make meaningful contributions.

As much as it may feel like an indulgence for some who are working only to put food on the table, there's no doubt that being able to do meaningful work – work that feels worthwhile and impactful – is an important contributor to our health and wellbeing.

The Covid-19 pandemic created an existential crisis that then became an existential opportunity. Because of the worldwide lockdowns, individuals and institutions started to think differently about work and how it gets done; working from home, remote working and hybrid working were all put on the agenda. But, perhaps more interestingly, people began to question the role and purpose of their work – and to look for more meaning in it. There's nothing like a global health emergency to put things into perspective!

In a world where economies are groaning and money is scarce, I'm now seeing in my clients a move away from intrinsic rewards being the biggest factor in taking or remaining in a job. There's a renewed emphasis on money and salary as major points of meaning, with the accompanying values of empathy, being supportive and being able to provide. There appears to be a growing balance of extrinsic and intrinsic motivators in many people's sense of values and meaning.

Aligning meaning and values

There are too many people in the world who are so blinded by the bling they can afford to buy with their salaries that they don't see how unhappy they are. Despite how this may sound, I say it with no judgement – but with an enormous amount of compassion for people who feel trapped in situation that's not rewarding them in any way other than financially.

Although making money, having fun and enjoying the time we spend at work is important, especially when we're young, feeling a sense of fulfilment and satisfaction from our work is perhaps even more significant. And it's hard to feel completely fulfilled and satisfied if we're doing work that holds no meaning for us, or that does not support our values.

It's also hard to find meaning in work that requires us to compromise our personal value system. This was a large part of the reason John (see page 102) felt such a high degree of aversion to his work. Although the organisation he was employed by was, ostensibly, delivering services in a manner that should have felt very meaningful and personally rewarding for him, the truth was that he was expected to go against his personal core values of integrity, empathy and honesty every day. It was the resistance to being expected to surrender his principles that created the aversion, not the work, which in other circumstances would have been very rewarding and consequential for John. Instead, he developed burnout from being expected to do things that were wrong – both in terms of the law and in terms of his own moral code – and his job became untenable.

On the other end of the spectrum are the people who have no issue with the values or morals of their job or workplace but find no meaning in what they're doing. These poor souls experience their work as so meaningless that it's draining and depressing, and this contributes to the burnout that arises from not doing enough of the right things, and from forcing oneself to stay in a situation that lacks any kind of satisfaction or significant reward.

One of the best ways to help you get better from despondency burnout is to find meaning in what we're doing. Even if it isn't in the actual day-to-day responsibilities of our work, it's useful to try to frame what we do in a way that feels meaningful. Making enjoyable connections with even one or two people in the office, or taking on some social-responsibility work, or starting a lunch club or a walking group with like-minded colleagues are all ways to find or create more meaning in what we're doing and how we're spending our time.

Jabu, like so many young graduates, had battled to find a job. At very long last, he was thrilled to be offered an internship. It was in a company for which he didn't feel any real affinity, and the pay was pretty minimal, but the position promised to provide him with the experience he so desperately wanted and needed to get a better job.

But, after a few months of largely menial labour, including photocopying and collating agendas, answering phones and setting up meeting rooms, Jabu was losing his enthusiasm to get out of bed in the morning to go to work. He was bored, and he felt as though he was neither making a meaningful contribution nor had he any opportunity to give back, which was one of his core values. Caught between the rock of work that wasn't making the most of his skills or training, and the hard place of no work at all, Jabu was in a pickle, and he was growing increasingly depressed and despondent.

We knew we had to keep him in that job for as long as possible so that he could get enough work experience to apply for jobs that would be more rewarding to him, so we started to explore ways that he could do something that felt important and value-aligned, and thus make his days at work feel less barren.

It turned out that Jabu was a voracious reader and was passionate about spreading the joy of reading to others. He lent every book he had the luxury of owning to friends and neighbours, and dreamed of setting up a community library that would make reading available on a much larger scale.

Jabu decided to speak to his supervisor about his dream, and to ask if there was anyone in the company who would be able to advise him on how to make it a reality. His supervisor, very aware of Jabu's boredom and under-utilisation, was thrilled to set up a meeting with the company's social responsibility officer and HR manager to see how they could help.

At that meeting it was agreed that Jabu would submit a proposal for his library idea. He had a lovely time coming up with his proposal, which included a budget for new books as well as a 'bring a book you loved' day when all staff members in the company were encouraged to donate books from home to the library. To his delight, not only was his proposal accepted, but the company decided to dedicate their next volunteering day to going to the community centre near Jabu's house and setting up a library of all the books they had bought and donated.

Jabu's library project took a few months to come to fruition, and the time and effort he put into it in his spare time at work made the admin tasks he'd been appointed to do feel much less menial and much more meaningful. To add to the joy of seeing his library materialise, Jabu gained additional, invaluable work experience in project management and community outreach, which helped him to get a job as a junior corporate social investment officer when his internship came to an end.

Few of us have the luxury of just stopping something that isn't making us happy. We have bills to pay, mouths to feed and stop orders to cover. I would never suggest anybody walk away from a job that's meeting their material needs in the absence of some other form of income. But I do know that forcing yourself to do something that makes you unhappy isn't only not worth it, it can be downright dangerous to your emotional, physical, relational, mental and spiritual health.

Even if you're not able to change the work that you're currently engaged in, you will be able to change some aspects of how you do your work.

When it comes to your values, ask yourself:

o   What are your core personal values? (If you struggle to think of your values, think about the person you identified as your Adult role model (on page 38) and anyone else you admire and respect, and identify the values you think they embody.)

o   How are you expressing your core values in a way that is most appropriate to where you are in your life right now? What are you doing to bring your core values to life?

o   Does your work currently allow you to express your values and/or find meaning in what you do?

o   What could you do to make your work a better expression of your values?

When it comes to meaning, ask yourself:

o   What holds meaning for you? What activities, tasks, events, conversations, etc (at and outside of work) feel most significant and rewarding to you?

o   What three things do you find most meaningful and impactful in your life? (e.g. creating, giving, learning, teaching, providing for your family) Are they extrinsic or intrinsic?

- ○ Have you ever had work (paid or unpaid – perhaps you volunteer/ed somewhere) that felt totally meaningful, rewarding and in alignment with your values? What was/is it? What did you value the most about it?
- ○ Are you currently doing work that you find meaningful? If so, in what way is it meaningful to you?
- ○ If you're not finding your work meaningful, what can you do to help yourself find meaning at work? Can you – individually or through your organisation – find a way to make a contribution to a worthy cause? Do you or can you create rewarding relationships and community at work?

Being mindful of your own values and aware of what feels meaningful or significant in your life and in your work will help you to make – or find – work that works better for you. Whether it's meaningful enough for you to make the money needed to support yourself and your family, or is more existential and intrinsic than that, when you're able to find or create some meaning for yourself in or at your work, you'll be taking an important step in making work work for you.

ADDING THE VALUE(S) YOU WANT TO SEE AT WORK

One of the ways that we can make work feel more meaningful is to add value to it.

Many of the case studies presented in this book illustrate the different ways we can add value to work by changing how we show up at work. Jabu did this by starting a very effective and impactful corporate social investment programme through his community library. Zara added value to her team and the broader organisation by encouraging a feeling of inclusion through the personal check-ins she instituted, and growing from mistakes through her 'lessons learned' agenda item. By changing the way they communicated with their colleagues, Jane and Buhle also added enormous value to their workplaces.

When George asked for help and started to delegate, he gave his colleagues the opportunity to step up and to get different experience and, most importantly, he taught them all the value of spending their energy wisely. Shireen added value by modelling being honest, open and vulnerable about her menopause journey, demystifying it for all her colleagues. And Brenda showed how powerful compassion and empathy can be in getting the most out of people.

These are just a handful of examples of what coaches see over and over again: when clients work on themselves, the people around them also benefit. Every client I've worked with who made a change to make work feel more meaningful and work better for them has added value to their workplace as well.

Ask yourself:
○ What value have you added to your work by improving the quality of your own life?
○ What value would you like to add to your own life and to your work?

Work is not the only thing

One of the best ways to make work work for you is to make sure that it's an *aspect* of your life rather than the *whole* of your life.

I see too many clients who've spent too much time putting almost all of their energy and attention into their work and then, when work has to take a back seat for any of a range of reasons (burnout, sadly, being a big one), they have nothing on which to focus their energy and attention. When faced with the vacuum that's created when work is no longer a focal point, many people feel unmoored and untethered, and may experience depression and an even greater sense of disconnection and lack of meaning.

We've all heard awful stories of people who've worked hard their whole lives and then, when their long-awaited retirement arrives, either die prematurely of a stress-related illness or get very depressed and unhappy and are unable to enjoy what was meant to be a time of rest and adventure. We've also seen (or been) people who are miserable on holiday because they don't have any hobbies or sporting interests or friendships to channel their energy into and on which to spend their holiday time.

When we place all or too much time and emphasis on finding meaning in our work, it isn't just our health that suffers. The rest of our life also diminishes and, in time, begins to feel less satisfying – which makes us look to work more for meaning in a vicious cycle of working more and living less.

Work can't (and shouldn't) be the only place we find meaning and value, or where we express ourselves. Ask yourself:
- What is important to you outside of your work?
- Are you paying enough attention to it? If not, how can you enhance the expression of your meaning and values outside of work?

Although it may not feel like it now, work is not the most or only important thing in your life. The more attention you pay to the other elements of your life, the more you'll enjoy your work, and the less you'll rely on your work to be the only thing that makes you happy.

Despite what society and your boss might tell you, and even if you are your own boss, work is not the only or even the most important thing in your life; it's just one element in our complex and wonderful personal ecosystem.

A healthy ecosystem

We tend to think of our work, our relationships, our health and our growth as being *different parts* of our lives – each a standalone element that can be kept apart in the same way that we separate our laundry washes into lights and darks. But just as we are whole beings made up of many facets that all influence and are influenced by each other, so our lives are a complex system of relationships that make up our physical and social environments. Each element in our individual ecosystem has its own purpose and role, and contributes to the overall health, wellbeing, balance and meaning of our lives.

Family, friends, studies, hobbies, health, sleep, exercise, travel – all these (and more) make up the ecosystem of which our work is also an integral part. Our work affects and is affected by what is going on in the rest of our world. We can't expect to do our best work when the rest of our life is out of whack. We can't expect to live our best, most meaningful life when our work is out of whack.

When our ecosystem is healthy and in balance, all the different elements cooperate to support each other and the whole, but when our ecosystem is out of balance, dis-ease can creep in and make our life a less happy and fulfilling place to be.

When we're under pressure, we prioritise the area of our life that's most demanding and urgent at that moment – often at the expense of other elements in our ecosystem, which will at some point in the future become the area most in need of our attention.

Having a well-rounded life means we have the opportunity to do the things that replenish the energy we spend and allow us to build and maintain our resilience for a sustainable, rewarding and meaningful time on earth.

BUILDING A HEALTHY ECOSYSTEM

You can only really do well at work – and indeed in the rest of your life – when all aspects of your ecosystem are healthy and supporting each other.

It's helpful to have a clear picture of your own personal ecosystem: where and how everything fits together, where it's out of balance, and what you need to be paying more attention to or spending less energy on.

Just as the Wheel of Work (see page 5) helped you to identify the areas of your work life that are (or were) less than optimal, a Wheel of Life can help you to see where your ecosystem is out of balance.

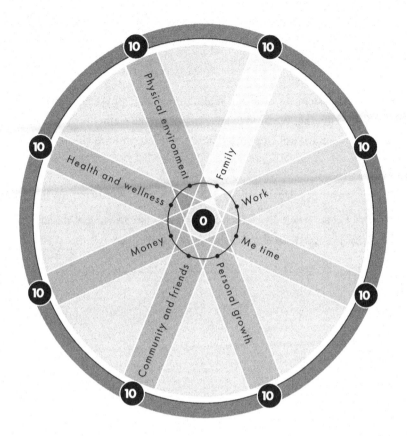

Draw your own Wheel of Life, then rate your current level of satisfaction in each of the life areas and join the dots to see where your personal ecosystem is out of balance and needs some attention.

Ask yourself:

o   Where do you need to be paying more attention (the elements that restore and generate energy for you)?

o   Where you need to be pulling back if possible (from the things that drain you)?

o   How is your work affecting and being affected by the other elements of the ecosystem?

o   What do you need to do to ensure that your work is a healthy and balanced aspect in your greater system?

When one or more elements is out of whack, the different elements cooperate to support each other and the whole. When something is out of balance, the whole ecosystem is compromised.

A healthy ecosystem is vital to maintaining our physical, emotional and professional wellbeing. We need to pay attention to all elements of our ecosystem to ensure that we are well supported and cared for, and are able to do our best work.

Can you think of two or three 'tiny' habits that will help you to improve your level of satisfaction in this area and make your Wheel of Work able to give you smoother ride?

Making work work for you

Just as we all have a survivor self – a part of us that keeps us safe and makes sure that we do whatever we need to do in order to stay relevant and alive – I believe we also have a succeeder self. Our succeeder self is that part of us that manages to navigate workplace politics – that knows what we're capable of and makes sure we get there, that smashes through the glass ceilings we encounter – in order to take us to the levels of success we are not only capable of, but deserve. It is the part of us that not only allows us to have a vision for our work and our life, but helps us to achieve that vision, through proper planning and mindfulness.

It's helpful to have a picture in your mind and even your wall of your succeeder self.

Have a vision

Too many of my clients pursue jobs and careers that they less than love but feel they need to stick it out because they've made a choice and feel they have to stick with it, or because they don't see any other options, or because their forefathers and parents didn't have the same opportunities that we do now. I see clients who do work that bores or frustrates them, that scares them or that leaves them cold, just because they think it is expected of them. Alignment of meaning and values, community at work and enjoying the working day all seem like a foreign language in a foreign country.

One absolute truism is that nothing in life is certain; life is precarious and unpredictable, and we should all be striving to do the things that make us happy and help us feel that one day we'll leave behind the legacy of a life well lived. Building that legacy starts now.

There are very few, if any, stories of people becoming wildly successful and leading lives of meaning through sheer luck. The vast majority of successful people – probably all – have got to where they are by having a vision or a goal of where they want to be, being mindful and deliberate about how they will achieve that goal, and effectively managing their resources, including their time and energy.

It's much simpler to get to where you want to be when you know what 'where you want to be' looks like. When you have a clear picture of the place, content and form of your ideal work, it will be easier to make choices that lead you towards that destination.

Now is the time to get clear and specific about your vision for your work and your life. Think back on all insights and realisations you've had over the course of reading this book and – without overthinking or editing yourself– complete the following sentences:

o   My ideal work has a physical environment that looks and feels...
o   My perfect work stimulates me by...
o   My conducive communities of and at work consist of...
o   I'm able to practise my super-power and strengths by...
o   When my work ecosystem is in balance, it looks like...
o   I'm recognised and feel noticed and appreciated at work through...
o   I give expression to my values and find meaning at work by...

With that vision in mind, you can weigh up all opportunities that come your way by asking yourself, 'If I do this thing, will it take me closer towards or further away from where I want to be?'

If doing it will take you closer to, or even keep you parallel with your vision, then it's worth considering. But if doing it is going to take you further away from where you want to be, then don't waste any more time or energy thinking about it.

Set aside an hour or so for this exercise. Collect some pens and pencils and find a quiet space where you won't be disturbed or interrupted, and allow your creative juices to flow.

Close your eyes so that you can visualise your succeeder self in as much detail as possible. Now ask yourself:
o   What sorts of clothes do they wear?
o   What does their hair look like?
o   What does their body look like?
o   Where do they live?
o   Who do they live with?
o   How do they present themselves to the world?
o   What work do they do?
o   Where is their work?
o   Who are their colleagues?

Once you have a pretty clear picture of your succeeder self, do a little sketch of them using your non-dominant hand (studies have shown than when we write or draw with our non-dominant hand, we access a part of our brain that allows us to be very creative and adventurous). Draw as detailed and exciting a picture of your succeeder self as you would like. Enjoy the process, and take as long as you need. Go into as much detail as you would like.

Once you've completed your succeeder self-portrait, have a conversation with them. Start the conversation by using your dominant hand to write a question to your succeeder self. Then transfer the pen to your non-dominant hand to allow your succeeder self to answer the question.

Your questions could include:

- o What are you most proud of yourself for achieving?
- o What are your hopes and dreams?
- o Where do you want to be in five years' time?
- o What do you need from me to get to where you want to be?
- o What do you need from others to get to where you want to be?
- o Do you have any advice or guidance for me now?

Once you start the conversation between your dominant hand and your non-dominant hand (representing your succeeder self), you'll be amazed at the insights and ideas that come out. This conversation will undoubtedly help you to create a plan to achieve the vision you have for yourself.

Make a plan

A vision is just a dream unless we plan to realise it. In 1973, time-management specialist Alan Lakein said in his book, *How to Get Control of Your Time and Your Life*, 'Planning is bringing the future into the present so that you can do something about it now.'

Planning isn't as scary or complex as many of us fear. Anyone who can get the kids to school in the morning or themselves to work on time is already a champion project manager. We all have lots of experience with making and carrying out plans of action: from cooking a meal, to submitting a research report, to pulling off a successful conference, life is a series of projects that we're mostly planning and executing without even thinking about it. A major part of what makes these projects successful is an innate knowing of what needs to be done, why it needs to be done, how it should happen, who should be involved, and where and when the tasks should be worked on.

The reason so many projects or plans fail in their execution is not because of lack of understanding or commitment, but because they're not adequately communicated to or supported by the people who are central to making the plan succeed. We don't pay enough attention to the upfront communication and collaboration required to make a plan come to life. Time and time again, I see well-laid plans failing because people don't explain them well enough or think to ask for help in making them happen.

Cast your mind and your eye back over all the notes you've made while you've been working through this book. Write down all the changes (big or small) that you've identified as being necessary to improve your experience of work, and that get you closer to the future you desire.

Now detail the steps you need to take in order to bring about these changes and make work work for you. For every action you've identified, ask yourself:

o   Why is this action important? You will need to know this so that you can communicate it effectively and convincingly.

o   Who do you need to ask for help or input, and why are these people appropriate? The people you should speak to will vary, depending on the nature of the action you want to take, and could include family (if you're thinking of making a big change), friends (maybe they can help you with networking), your manager or boss, your colleagues, or a recruitment specialist.

o   What do you want to say to your helpers? Be clear about what you would like help with. Try not to be apologetic, and explain your request clearly and in an uncomplicated way.

o   How do you want to express yourself? Think about the best way to communicate with each identified person. Summon up your calm, rational, empowered Adult self to both plan what to then say, and to then say it.

o   Where and when do you want to speak to the helpers? Timing and location of conversations are very important to their outcome, as anyone who's tried to have an important conversation with someone who's watching their favourite programme on TV knows!

Sometimes we feel too proud to ask for help. Sometimes we feel too scared to ask for help. And sometimes it just doesn't occur to us to ask for help. But asking for help – as scary as it may seem – is the single most powerful thing you can do to get you plan working and your dream living.

Once you've asked for help or input from even one person, you'll see how easy it is to gain traction with making your plan a reality. You'll feel supported and held – and you'll also feel more accountable to follow through on your plans.

Planning and prioritising go hand in hand, and are essential to achieving our goals successfully.

When we plan effectively, we can get more done, feel and be less anxious and stressed, focus on our tasks, and perform better, so that we're able to enjoy more downtime outside of work and lead healthier and happier lives. In order to effectively plan – and execute our plans – we need to be able to prioritise. Most of us spend the majority of our time on the most urgent, but not always the most important tasks, while we should be spending most of our time on the tasks that are important but not yet urgent.

The Eisenhower Matrix, made famous by Stephen Covey, the author of the 1989 bestseller, *The 7 Habits of Highly Effective People*, is a really useful model to help us understand how and why we fail to effectively get things done, and to assist us to prioritise our time and attention so that we can achieve our goals. This table gets its name from US president Dwight D Eisenhower, who famously said, 'I have two kinds of problems, the urgent and the important.'

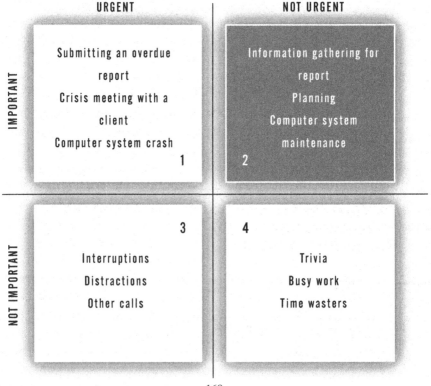

	URGENT	NOT URGENT
IMPORTANT	Submitting an overdue report Crisis meeting with a client Computer system crash **1**	Information gathering for report Planning Computer system maintenance **2**
NOT IMPORTANT	**3** Interruptions Distractions Other calls	**4** Trivia Busy work Time wasters

- **Quadrant 1**: important and urgent. This contains tasks that have immediate and important deadlines (e.g. marking tests, getting a proposal in, attending to a critically ill patient, going to the doctor for a high fever).
- **Quadrant 2**: important but not urgent. This is for long-term strategising and development (e.g. lesson plans for the year ahead, consulting stakeholders for input on upcoming plans and proposals, giving children their inoculations, exercising regularly).
- **Quadrant 3**: urgent but not important. This is for time-pressured distractions – they aren't really important, but someone wants them now (e.g. calls from parents or managers, demands for attention from patients who are healthy but lonely, buying items on special offer before the sale ends).
- **Quadrant 4**: not urgent and not important. This is for those activities that yield little, if any value, and are often used for taking a break between time-pressured and important activities (e.g. spending time on social media, playing endless rounds of computer solitaire, making another unnecessary cup of tea).

In an ideal world, we would all be putting most of our attention on the items in quadrant 2 – the things that are important but not yet urgent – thus ensuring that life is calm and measured at all times. But when we're overwhelmed or exhausted, or even just not paying attention, we stop being proactive and instead become reactive – fighting fires that have ignited as a result of not being given attention.

When we can't or don't plan effectively, the things that are important will inevitably become urgent, and we'll have to spend most of our time attending to quadrant 1 in order to avoid disaster. And the more time we spend in quadrant 1, the less time we have to allocate to quadrant 2, ensuring that more and more tasks are moving from quadrant 2 to quadrant 1 – from 'important but not urgent' to 'important and urgent'.

We become so exhausted and frazzled by living in a state of reaction and crisis management that when we do have a small break, instead of addressing quadrant 2, we generally head straight to quadrant 4 – not urgent and not important – and do mindless, comforting and totally unproductive things.

There's nothing wrong with having some downtime, but when we tell ourselves that we're being productive when in fact we're surfing Instagram, then we're doing the work equivalent of eating empty calories. We're merely wasting precious time that will result in our having to crank up the adrenaline to manage the imminently urgent and important tasks that we're avoiding. And when we enter into that adrenaline-fuelled state of panic, we're unable to differentiate between the things that are important and urgent, and those that are unimportant and urgent – reacting to both and wasting even more time solving things that have no real bearing on our performance.

Use this matrix to help you spend your time and energy wisely, by allocating the items on your task list to the various quadrants (www.developgoodhabits.com/eisenhower-matrix).

	URGENT	NOT URGENT
IMPORTANT	**1** **Do**	**2** **Plan**
NOT IMPORTANT	**3** **Delegate**	**4** **Eliminate**

The only way to ensure that we're paying enough attention to the important things is to plan properly. Remember that planning isn't scary or difficult; we're planning all the time, even when it doesn't feel like we are.

Mindfulness

Being mindful allows us to be purposeful and productive.

The busier we are, the less mindful we become. The less mindful we are, the less effective we are. And the less effective we are, the more likely it is that we'll push ourselves into exhaustion and burnout.

The more mindfully we start and end our days, the more likely we are to get more done, without getting burnout. It may seem like a big ask – especially when you're stressed and stretched for time, but I can assure you that the more present we are with ourselves, the calmer, kinder and more effective we become in our lives.

Plan your week ahead: write a to-do list that's a combination of big and small tasks, urgent and not urgent, important and not important.

Every morning, plan your day: write a to-do list that's also a combination of big and small tasks, urgent and not urgent, important and not important.

Finish your day mindfully
You can end your day well and ensure that you start the next day well by spending 5-10 minutes reviewing your task list every day before you leave your desk. Give yourself a pat on the back for achieving what you got done (you can even write a 'got-done' list). If you didn't manage to do everything you'd hoped to, think about how you can do things differently tomorrow.

Finish each day in a mood of appreciation of yourself and all you've completed!

The more mindful we can be about our responses and reactions to the situations we find ourselves in, the more effective we can be, and the more we can make life and work work for us – and everyone around us.

Having worked through this book, I suggest that you repeat the Wheel of Work exercise and see if you've made any changes to how you feel about your work. It's really effective to go back to your original drawing and, using a different coloured pen, overlay your updated Wheel of Work on it for a visual representation of what has (or hasn't) changed as a result of reading the various chapters.

You'll probably notice that you've allocated slightly higher scores in some of the areas, and slightly lower scores in others. There may be a universal improvement or a universal decline – it's all important information for where you need to be paying attention and allocating your time and energy. It's also helpful in identifying where and how you may be holding yourself back from the success you deserve.

The hope is that now you will have a picture of where your Wheel of Work is out of alignment, as well as some knowledge and understanding – and practical tools – to panelbeat it back into shape. Some adjustments will be easier to make and to keep up than others, but any actions you take, no matter how big or small, will help you to gain momentum to make your work work better for you, and get you closer to where you want to be in your career.

If you've made even one improvement to just one of the eight areas, you'll already be experiencing a slightly smoother ride at work. Perhaps your relationships feel more enriching, or you're feeling more equipped to say 'no' to what you can't do, or you feel more able to ask for help where you need it. Maybe you're enjoying the changes you've made to your physical space, or are feeling healthier as a result of the increased fresh air and hydration you're giving yourself. I'm almost certain you're more self-aware, and are managing to communicate effectively and powerfully from your Adult ego state.

Whatever tiny changes you've been able to implement, you'll soon start to see a ripple effect; those tiny changes will start to radiate out into other areas of your work experience – and to your colleagues. One of the things I love most about introducing these ideas to clients is watching the alchemy that happens in their lives and the lives of the people around them as a result. The changes we make for ourselves very quickly become exponential.

My aim is to help the people I work with to improve their experience and quality of life by making changes – not to *who* they are but to *how* they are, because how we are not only profoundly affects, but also has a profound effect on, our experience of the world.

I hope this book has helped you to change how you are at work and to make your work work for you – not just now, but in your future work, too.

Acknowledgements

This book is the result of countless hours of coaching the many clients I've been lucky enough to work with. It builds on the life lessons from my two previous books, *Recover From Your Childhood: Life Lessons for the Adult Child* and *Recover From Burnout: Life Lessons to Regain your Passion and Purpose.*

It would not have been possible without the support that came from many sources:

- The team at Bookstorm: Tracey, Janet, Nicola and especially Louise who has believed in my books from the very beginning.
- My family and friends, who have graciously borne the boredom of my preoccupation with the thoughts, ideas, structure and everything else that is involved in a project of this nature. I won't name them all because it's an extremely long list but I must mention Sarah for her insightful suggestions, Barbara for her drawings and Jenny who was instrumental in ensuring that I sat still for long enough to get the words down, while being the voice of reason whenever I felt like giving up.
- Special thanks to Stephen, who is not only a sounding board but also a springboard for me.
- The clients who have not only shared their experiences with me but graciously agreed to have their stories in the book.